# SAHARAN SAFARI

We took our VW Camper on a freighter to Morocco 1969-70 This is the story of our adventures for ten months. Our only help came from our research and guide books purchased in New York and Casablanca.

## Ted Jones
## and
## Emma Selig Jones

iUniverse, Inc.
Bloomington

# SAHARAN SAFARI

We took our VW Camper on a freighter to Morocco 1969-70 This is the story of our adventures for ten months. Our only help came from our research and guide books purchased in New York and Casablanca.

iUniverse books may be ordered through booksellers or by contacting:

iUniverse
1663 Liberty Drive
Bloomington, IN 47403
www.iuniverse.com
1-800-Authors (1-800-288-4677)

ISBN: 978-1-4759-4243-9 (sc)
ISBN: 978-1-4759-4244-6 (ebk)

Printed in the United States of America

iUniverse rev. date: 08/13/2012

# CONTENTS

# DEDICATION

A TRIBUTE TO THE AUTHOR TED JONES WHO PASSED
AWAY MAY 26, 2012, JUST AFTER COMPLETEING
HIS THIRD BOOK

TED AND I WERE MARRIED 66 YEARS AND I AM FORTUNATE
TO HAVE BEEN PARTNERS WITH HIM AS HE LIVED OUT HIS
ADVENTUROUS SPIRIT

EMMA S. JONES

# INTRODUCTION

The following pages relate the travels and adventures starting in Casablanca, Morocco to the central part of the Sahara in Ain Salah, Algeria. We travelled for ten months in a VW Camper. The VW Camper made it possible to travel slowly and in relative comfort.

Ignorant people and ill planned forays into the Sahara have, as should be expected, given the desert the reputation of being what it is, dangerous. Our maps and guide books, especially Michelin maps were extremely helpful in locating wells with a supply of potable water, including the number of feet needed for a rope to reach the water supply. Most wells were 100 feet or more down. The maps were very necessary because of the limited supply of wells containing potable water.

The Algerian Government has done, and is doing everything possible to protect the desert traveler. The authorities in every village are in constant radio contact but they must know you are there and where you are headed. Traveling in convoy is, at times, required for the safety of the traveler but, it can be a nuisance, a hindrance to one's freedom, often the reasoning for traveling in the desert.

The five north south desert tracks are not race ways. The goal is to observe the desert and its life forms not to determine how fast it is possible to cross it. Life in the desert has to be secretive to survive. Predators are determined and crafty hunters, survivors are expert at camouflage. It is very difficult to observe desert dwellers in action. Their life experiences must be read each morning in the sand, around every rock, bush, and tuft of grass. People who travel fast cover lots of the desert but they actually see little or nothing.

It is a life experience to set up camp just before sunset. Then watch and feel the desert atmosphere change as the chill of night arrives and the stars emerge with a brilliance beyond description. It is very interesting, tempting to wander off into the dunes at night, but it is wiser to wait until morning and read the events of the night in the sand.

All life forms must adapt to the desert environmental changes as they occur over millions of years. In order to survive and establish an ecological balance all plants, animals and men must adapt, migrate if possible or die.

Throughout the Sahara there is evidence of ancient camps that were set up along rivers, streams and lakes. It is fascinating to observe the remains of those camps, and speculate upon who might have lived there, how did they survive, where did they come from and where did they go. A Saharan Safari should include an anthropologist, a geologist, a desert ecologist and an experienced Taureg guide.

The ancient history of the Sahara, its formation and evolution through many millions of years is plainly written in the basic rock foundation and the story of past volcanic action. In the disintegration of the original granite and crystalline rock, their disintegration to form sand seas, sand stone and the constant cycle that has taken place. The action of desert sand and wind of rivers, streams, lakes and seas form a, first class real-life mystery. But, it is not a novel, It is the real-life story of evolution in one small part of the planet The Algerian Sahara.

# CASABLANCA TO MARRAKESH

It was 1969; we were living in the village of Meshoppen, Pennsylvania. Emma was to start work as a Guidance Counselor the following year—I had retired from teaching biology at Georgia Tech and was building, and renting apartments. We had traveled in North, South, and East Africa—But never in the Sahara! We had about a year free and we decided to make the break.

We soon learned that you do not just buy a ticket, hop on a ship and head for Africa! Emma took on the job of handling the paper work. Getting the VW Camper in shape for such an undertaking, fell upon me. Passage on the freighter had to be secured—A Carnet for the vehicle—Passports brought up to date—Clothing and supplies selected. The paper work required many hours. Extra fuel and water tanks were required, two extra spare tires added, automotive spare parts purchased—Preparation required weeks. Finally, the phone rang—The Yugoslav Freighter was docking in Brooklyn—The camper should be loaded and we must head for port. The destination was Casablanca! That sounded exciting!

Loading the vehicle turned out to be a problem. The dock workers could not understand the shift pattern—And they did not want anyone else to drive the vehicle! After considerable haggling I was allowed to position the vehicle so that it could be hoisted aboard. Then they stowed it on the deck! More discussion finally got the vehicle covered securely with a canvass. It also had to be lashed down securely in case of a storm at sea—And there was one! Now we could relax and check out the other passengers—But first we had to get aboard!

We clambered up the steep and narrow gangplank with several of our bags and boxes—The crew members carried the rest to our stateroom. It was very plain, but neat and clean. Our goal was to get to Casablanca and the Sahara—We did not expect a cruise on the QE!!

As we settled in we became aware of the loading—And over the next two days and nights the cranes ran constantly!! Well, we said, we can sleep after we leave port. The holds fore and aft were filled to the very top—There certainly would not have been room for the camper—And if there had been there would have been great danger that some cargomight shift—That would have been the end of our journey!!

We finally met all the passengers at the first breakfast. Several were from Yugoslavia—They had visited relatives in the U.S. None of them spoke any English—But then, neither did either of us speak Slavic!! The Captain knew a few words in English but none of the officers or Crew spoke English! Emma and I would be talking to each other like we never did before!!

In addition to the Yugoslav passengers there were five young Americans. They spoke to each other and to us only when questioned. They spent a lot of time in the bar—Well, so did I trying to find out why they were heading for Casablanca—And with very little baggage! We had plenty of time and tried not to press them too hard. Slowly, we learned that they were going to Casablanca to buy dope! A little closer observation indicated that they would soon need a new supply

As the days passed and we all headed for the dining room we noticed that one of the passengers was always there first, and waiting. He never looked at anything except the food—And he never was served enough! My professional diagnosis: He had a tapeworm several feet long!

Several days out the ocean started to get rough, then it got rougher, and then it got rougher still! All the furniture that was not attached was thrown about. It was not possible to move without holding onto something. One elderly man was knocked down; he broke his arm and required first aid until we got to Casablanca. During the storm the Captain ordered a head-count of the passengers—One of the five boys was missing! The ship was rolling very badly—The waves were crashing over the bow! Everyone who could; searched for the young man. His friends were of no help—They all had been taking, or shooting, something—The storm did not seem to bother them. After several hours had passed the Captain announced, as best he could, that the young man had been located—He had been up in the bow of the ship trying to fly—And he fell into the anchor hole! Fortunately he had been holding his arms out in order to fly—And that kept him from falling through and into the Atlantic Ocean.

The ocean slowly began to calm down.—So did the passengers! But the ship did not! It rolled constantly from side to side—And the furniture kept sliding around. Everyone adjusted to it—It was not a subject of conversation. Of course there was little conversation in any event! The ship obviously did not have stabilizing fins—In fact; the ship did not seem to have anything not absolutely required for sailing! Our main concern was getting to Casablanca—For a while we thought that we might not make it—Especially when the ship rolled on its side and you could look straight down into the ocean.

After ten days at sea we put into the port of Casablanca! Emma and I stood at the railing and watched our camper being unloaded. At one point it shifted and we stopped breathing! But the crane operator was skillful and he righted it almost instantly.

As we stood there at the railing Emma squeezed my arm and said," We are back in Africa!" We had ten months of freedom to travel almost as we wished! The excitement is impossible for me to describe! Now we could head across Morocco to the Algerian border! First we had to disembark. An Arab who spoke perfect English came aboard. Our papers were in perfect order—Many thanks to Emma. The Yugoslav passengers, of course stayed aboard. But we knew that the Hippies had planned to disembark in order to buy their dope. The interpreter explained that there was a meeting of the Hippies with the Captain. They were at the railing, as we were, when we docked. They saw all the Arabs wearing their red hats and robes! The cultural shock was just too much! They wanted to remain on the ship and go home. Normally the Captain might not allow such a maneuver—But the young fellows were in such a state that he agreed to allow them to remain aboard, go on to Yugoslavia, and return to New York. Emma and I wondered—What about their dope supply? Well, we thought, maybe they would be able to buy a supply right there in Casablanca?? It would be a long trip home without it—We never found out

We sailed through customs and finally we were foot-loose in Casablanca! Hunger pangs became quite apparent and we wanted to find a place to eat. However, when we had time to look at the inside of the camper we realized that food would have to wait—The inside of the camper was a jumbled mess! Everything had been fastened to something—But in spite of our precautions, during the storm all our supplies seemed to have been put through a blender. Some semblance of order had to be restored. I found a place to park under a tree and we went to work. The extra fuel cans had to be hooked on each side—The water containers had to be fastened to the roof rack—All the cooking equipment had to be re-stowed—Even the window curtains had to be reattached! And, after Emma restored some semblance of order, she had to clean the floor while I checked the tire rack and the motor. After what seemed like several hours we decided that the rest would have to wait—We had to find food!

On our way to the Medina, not far from the clock-tower we found, what turned out to be a great place for couscous—It was a little too hot for me—But it tasted delicious! While we were eating an Arab man started talking to us about the major sites in Casablanca. We not only learned not to miss the Hassan II Mosque, the Villenouvelle around Place Mohamed V, and the Maureesque architecture,—He also recommended the beaches, and the Medina.

Along with the tour information we were given a rather thorough history of Morocco and of Casablanca. It made us think—We would never be able to give such detailed information to an Arab tourist visiting in the U.S.!

We followed his advice on the Medina—The old Arab part of the city. There were crowds of people in every type dress imaginable! The shops were small but packed with all types of goods. Each section specialized in something—Shoes, porcelain dishes and plates, burnooses (robes) leather products. The very narrow streets were covered, making some areas rather dark. In the jewelry section Emma had several invitations to have tea. She accepted one. Everything went very well until the proprietor realized that she was not going to buy anything! He expressed part of his disappointment in English—And some of it in Arabic! We could understand how he felt—He, of course, could have no idea of how long we intended to travel, how far we had to go, and that our funds were very far from unlimited!!

The Medina was most interesting! They always are. It was similar to the old Arab towns and shopping areas that we had visited in Tunisia. But, it was getting late in the day and we had to find a place to camp. Casablanca is a city of well over five million. We made our way through very upscale Villas, along beautifully landscaped boulevards—And through some very depressing areas. The contrast, like that in the U.S. always is a very sobering experience. How do you limit the population, spread the wealth more equitably, and reduce some of the suffering? We felt very fortunate to be able to do what we were doing.

In one guide book the statement is made that the beaches west of town are nothing special. We have to take issue with that! We drove onto the white sand, had an almost unlimited view, there were very few people—We had the area practically to ourselves.

After the rather rough crossing, we thought it might be best to rest a bit. The days passed quickly. Emma prepared our meals on a one burner stove. The food was not lavish. That is not what we were there for. But it was tasty, and nourishing. (I better say that!)

Each day we walked along the beautiful white sand of the Atlantic Ocean. I developed quite an appetite it was necessary to drive into the nearest market for additional supplies. Shopping was not a problem—Every type store that one might need was relatively easy to locate.

When we set up camp on the beach we did think of some of the less prosperous areas we ad passed through. Might some of those people who frequent the beach be around? We did not see any—We had no interference. We had to move on, leave the beach, but we were really not happy about it. The Sahara kept calling! We were to learn that not only is it a long way across Morocco—But there is infinite beauty to see and try to photograph! Far too much to take in by driving one time! Figuig, the Moroccan—Algerian border station beckoned—and, without doing justice to Casablanca, we decided to head for Rabat.

Decisions were not made lightly—Usually! A conference of two was called. The maps were laid out on the kitchen table, mileage was calculated, roads and passes considered . . . The VW had forty horsepower—That was only when all four cylinders were firing, the valves were set properly, and the fuel was at least combustible. The air filter also had to be checked, the dust knocked out and oil added. It was also necessary to check the transmission and the reduction gears on the rear wheels! Well, everything seemed to check out—We headed for Marrakech.

In spite of our plans, we first headed north-east—We wanted to see Rabat, the capitol. Then, along the road, we decided to do that on the return trip. There was open country—But, it was strange country to us. The truth is that we were nervous—Unsure of how the owner of the land might react. It turned out that finding a campsite was not the problem. All we needed was to be able to get off the road. Traffic was very light to non-existent.

The problem was trying to make the Arab owner understand what it was that we wanted to do. He could not get the idea that we wanted to park and sleep in the vehicle. He sent for assistance. At that point there were two Arabs, many children, Emma and I, all talking at once—And speaking Arabic, French, and English!!

In desperation Emma opened the camper doors, put up the folding table, pulled out the bed and laid down as if to sleep! You could see the lights go on! Everyone laughed and took a long look at the inside of the camper—It was a thorough inspection. They understood what we wanted to do and there was absolutely no problem. They made it very clear that we were welcome, could stay as long as we wished.

By then it was quite dark, we were more tired than hungry. The men chased all the children, we went straight to bed and slept vary soundly. After a good nights sleep, Emma made breakfast—Oatmeal! Well, it did taste very delicious! (It is necessary that I frequently make such comments.)

Another top-level conference was convened—It was discovered that we did not have a Visa for Algeria!! That would prove to be a first-order disaster! We had talked to several travelers and were given to understand that we would not get over the border without a Visa—And perhaps not with one!!

We turned around, headed back to Casablanca, turned right, and headed up the coast toward Rabat. Fortunately, we told each other, we had plenty of time—We had about ten months of free time ahead of us. That turned out not to be true. Time ran out In the Sahara, it got very hot—And we had to make a dash to the north! But now we were headed up the coast and, as usual, looking for a camping place.

We did, on occasion, go into a regular campground. They were clean, pleasant, friendly, and reasonable. But when we were on the move it was easier to just pull off the road for the night. We never had any serious trouble.

The main road from Casablanca to Rabat was straight and in excellent condition. Not far out of Casa. We found a view point. There was plenty of room and we found a place on the side where we would be as inconspicuous as possible. The view over the Atlantic was beautiful.

Making camp was very simple—We never placed anything outside in order not to attract attention. As far as anyone passing by we simply appeared to be parked and enjoying the view—And they would be right on both counts.

Every time we stopped in the evening I ran a quick check of the camper. We were having no apparent mechanical problems—And we wanted to avoid any! Since we had an air-cooled engine there was no problem in that department. The oil and air filters had been checked—We were not burning oil and the fan belt tension was OK.

We were just starting out and we wanted to catch any problems while we had ready access to VW repair shops—And there were plenty as far south as Marrakech. Of course we were apprehensive, the 1961 camper had many thousands of miles on it—But, it did have a new motor!

We sat at the fold-up table, checked the map into Rabat and went to bed—And to sleep. We very rarely had trouble sleeping. We just did not see or hear anything that we could worry about. Of course, there is the real possibility that neither of us had sense enough to worry. Either way—It was not a problem!

# RABAT, MOROCCO

In the morning after breakfast of eggs and bacon we cranked up the VW and headed on down the road and into Rabat. It should be understood that we were traveling at the speed of 35 to 40 miles per hour. We could travel far—But not fast. At any rate, the one big advantage was that at 40 miles per hour there is time for sightseeing.

The entrance was via Route De Casablanca (I think) Anyway, it led into Avenue Hassan 11. There were flower gardens all over the place! It was similar to Casa. Which also had beautiful gardens and trees in abundance? We thought either city would be pleasant to live in. The air would be clean. From the brief view that we had we thought that Rabat might be the better of the two. Casa. Had many multi-storied buildings, a huge port and a lot of traffic and activity.

Rabat had many beautiful buildings—We thought that we could detect the recent French occupation. But, it was the capitol, and had the administrative departments. We could appreciate the wide avenues, the trees and gardens, and the location by the ocean. Our lack of historical perspective became very apparent. At the very least, we should have had a brief history lesson on the people and geography! Well, we were ignorant and had to make the best of it!

The Medina came into view on our left and we found a parking place. The ancient walls are still standing, and they are beautiful! There is so much beauty and history to see and try to appreciate!

The Medina was crowded—And the streets were narrow. There were Arabs all over the place! That did not surprise us. Many shopping stall were open, and vendors and peddlers were numerous. We had a great time just walking around and looking at the hectic activity. All types of materials were being moved about—Some in carts pulled by donkeys—A lot of it on the backs of men and women. Still, when they passed us and we caught their eye at times they would smile. I would not be able to do that.

On down the avenue, along the Bou Regreg River, we came upon the Hassan Tower. This time by accident! We knew that it was in Rabat but did not know just where we were.

The tower seems Hugh. An English-speaking guide, or custodian, gave us some background information. (He did not want any money.) The tower is about 53 feet square. Its walls eight feet thick! I wondered if it had been designed to be cannon-proof! It is 144 feet high! We did not ask about climbing it. The guide said it had been closed for a time because of suicides—He was not certain. Anyway, it was not something that we had in mind. It was constructed at the end of the 18th century. It was part of a Hugh mosque. The guide said it was large enough to accommodate an army for prayers.

The work was never completed. Some of the columns are still standing. Inside there are several rooms and a series of ramps leading to the top. The ramps accommodated pack animals carrying stone and building materials to the top. I did not want to walk to the top! Those pack-animals more than earned their keep!

The attendant told us not to miss visiting Sale across the river. He related some of its history. We really appreciated his information—Too bad we did not have room to take him with us! We had seen The Great Mosque and the Royal Palace (From the outside.) We were very tired of sight-seeing. It was a lot of information to try to digest. Once again we camped along the street.

While we were eating the stew that Emma made, (She only had one burner to cook on.) We talked about what we had seen—We had a lot to talk about. We had seen many of the cathedrals in Europe. Now we were seeing the Mosques in North Africa. We thought that it was interesting that, at about the same time in history, the Christians were building Cathedrals, the Arabs were building Mosques. And still, Emma said, they found plenty of time to fight amongst themselves and each other!! The living standards of the Christian and Arab craftsmen left a lot to be desired. The entire lives of the workmen, and their families were devoted to their work. "Well ", I told her, "I will have to take that under consideration at some later date ". We hit the sack—Another day, and Sale, were waiting—

Our "plan", if it could be called that, was to dash into Rabat, find the Algerian Embassy, pick up our visa, and continue our journey. That proved to be impossible—And, it would have been very unwise.

Rabat, like Casa, is a beautiful city full of outstanding areas of flower gardens and trees. (It warrants repetition!) In addition to that we encountered so many helpful people who spoke English—And took the time to give us some history relating to a particular park, monument, or gate. Each area, every standing wall, each Mosque, has its own unique, and fascinating history!

The second day we did make it to the Algerian Embassy. It was located in an area set aside for foreign legations. The outside of the building was attractive and well maintained. The Algerian Office inside was quite plain—Perhaps austere might describe it. The room into which we were ushered had almost no furniture. The walls were drab, undecorated.

There were no chairs. We stood in front of an uncluttered desk until a man in a very plain suit came in and sat down. He knew what we wanted. He spoke English, requested our passports with two extra small pictures and told us to return in two days. We found our way out.

The reason for the situation described above can be explained by the tension that has existed between Algeria and Morocco over the past several years. We were to see much more evidence of their disagreement in the near future!

On various occasions, in different countries we have experienced similar situations. When approached by any political group we quickly explain that we are tourists, we are "just looking", and we do not know enough to make any comment. And that is actually the truth.

Our lesson was learned the hard way many years ago in Tunisia. The French Foreign Legion was occupying the country. Our sympathy was with some poverty-stricken Arabs. It is best to keep a very low profile when one is uninformed, or, even worse, ill-informed!

Over the following two days we had time to drive around Rabat and Sale on the other side of the River Bou Regreg. Perhaps people on a tour bus can "do" Rabat in a day or an afternoon—We could not!

After locating the Post Office and checking our mail, we exchanged some dollars for dirhams, the local currency. There was a black market but the difference in rates was not worth the risk of getting involved.

From the bank we headed for the Medina, the ancient quarter of town. The Medina in Rabat is similar to that in Casa. But to say that if you have seen one you have seen them all would be very far from the truth. In words, or on film, it is impossible to capture the feeling, the aroma, and the atmosphere of the Souk, the Market, and the Medina.

The little shops had everything that any normal person might want, and a lot that he would not want. Each section had its specialty—Food, fruit and vegetables—Shoes, leather goods of every type—Copper and iron works—Pottery and ceramics—Jewelry—Far too many to see or list!

We wandered through the twisting, narrow streets—Being careful to keep out of the way of people carrying very heavy loads on their backs, of donkeys with packs on each side, one carrying lumber, and of bicycles and motor scooters

After several inquires, and having well-meaning people point us in the wrong direction, we arrived back at the entrance. We drove past the Royal Palace and the Great Mosque. We did not have the energy to get out of the camper! The beach was easy to locate on the map. It was between the Medina and the ocean. There was a wall along one side, we found a wide place along the wall and, "set up camp". In the morning we drove back along the river to the Bridge Hassan 11, across, and we were in Sale! There were many little ferries crossing but we didn't see anything that we wanted to put the camper on.

If we did not enjoy traveling we would not do it. There are so many other pursuits that are just as interesting. But, when you travel it is possible to see, and enjoy, a constantly changing panorama of the planet—Or at least a tiny part of it. The frustrating aspect is that there is so much to see and learn that it can become exasperating!

In traveling about in Sale it is impossible not to see, and be impressed by the ancient walls. Over the centuries of occupation they have been laboriously built, destroyed, and rebuilt! It makes one wonder.

The site of Sale has been occupied for thousands of years. Early man was there long before the first Berbers. Cro-Magnon traces of occupation have been found. Next in history came the Phoenicians, traders who navigated through the Mediterranean Sea and down the west coast of Africa. The Romans seem to have appeared next, followed by the Arabs in the 8th century. And the Berbers just adapted as the centuries went by.

The Berbers seem to be "forever". Over the centuries they have seen so-called "conquers" come and then fade into history.

We learned that around the 17th century many Arabs expelled from Spain were settled across the river in New Sale. Apparently, they were quite unhappy and formed what came to be called the "Sale Rovers". They harassed shipping as far north as Europe and made their home port very wealthy. They had a main purpose—To eventually take back the Iberian Peninsula! It was not to be. Robinson Caruso was captured by the "Sale Rovers". The details of that story escape me. At any rate, toward the end of the 18th century their activities faded into history. The fate of all mans activities! Camp was made in Sale one more night. There was a campground available but we elected not to use it. In the morning we headed for the Algerian Consulate. We did not know what to expect. From what we had heard, we expected almost anything.

Once again we followed the same ritual. There was practically no conversation. The same man appeared handed us our pass ports and surprise! He wished us a pleasant and safe journey! We wondered if he meant anything by "safe ". We had our visas for Algeria! (And we were going to need them!)

On the road south to Romani we had to stop for fuel. The old VW went many miles on ten gallons—But, with all the weight we were carrying, our mileage dropped. And the steep mountain climbs did not help. However, when we got down into first or second, We could almost climb up a wall! (Well, maybe not!)

# MARRAKESH

The good road went south and west into Marrakesh. As we drove along, The High Atlas Mountains were always in view. They are spectacular!

Rugged and snow-covered, it was easy to understand why they are so popular with tourists, hikers, and winter sports enthusiasts. The mountains are visible from Casa, and Rabat. They dominate the scenery—And the climate. There are several chains of mountains—The Rif runs along the Mediterranean Sea in the north—The Moyen Atlas is next to the south, then the High Atlas, and finally south to the desert and the Anti-Atlas Mountains. We camped on the street in Rabat for several days waiting for our Visa to Algeria

Morocco's rivers originate in those mountains, most of them drain into the Atlantic—One into the Med. To the south the drainage forms rivers that flow into the desert and form underground rivers. Some of them come to the surface in the desert and form beautiful, and welcome, oases!

South of the Cascades d Ouzoud we could see the Palmaris of Marrakech some of the ramparts are to be seen. Marrakesh, with its surrounding vast plain, its Palmaris, ramparts, distant snow-covered mountains, and well over a million inhabitants from the north and south of Africa, is unique! No wonder some people call it Morocco's jewel. It is that—And more!

Arrived we did not have time to sight-see. We needed to find a bank and exchange some money. That may be why tourists are welcome! We never needed to exchange large sums of money. Living in the VW made it possible to travel far on little. But it did have certain drawbacks—To some extent we were isolated from the people. The more contact you have with the natives, the more you learn. It is just that simple!

We were to learn that when we stopped at the American Express to check on our mail. There we met a Frenchman who spoke English much better than we did. Of course he also spoke Arabic—And French.

He was very helpful and helped us transact our business and then invited us to have tea with him the following morning at a nearby hotel. We gladly accepted. We made our way to the east end of town, located the Youth Hostel and nearby the Municipal Campsite. It was time for us to get some rest. If there was supposed to be a fee they did not charge us. It was possible to clean up a little better than when we camped along the road. Also, it was easier to work outside the camper and fill the water tanks.

The next morning we were waiting at the sidewalk café for our Frenchman friend. He was on time. He was very polite, but curious as to who we were, where we came from, and where we planned to go. We learned that he had lived in Marrakesh for many years. He was there when the French granted independence to Morocco in 1956. He admitted that he was quite nervous at that time—Especially because he had a native Moroccan wife. But, all went well; he had no trouble, probably because he was obviously an asset to the country.

When we asked him if he ever thought of leaving Morocco he made it quite clear "Never They would have to force me out—And we have no plans to ever leave Marrakech!" As we learned more about Marrakesh, and became familiar with the town, we could understand his feelings. He had no interest in returning to France.

The man was a fountain of information. We should have had a tape recorder—I am serious! We learned that Marrakesh was founded about 1062. But, there had been camps there long before that—Probably desert Berbers. Among all the Mosques that he listed, the famous Koutoubia was frequently mentioned. He told us about the many Arab Leaders who have reined over the centuries. Many more than I can remember—and their names, to me, are impossible!

If I have gained any concept of Arab History, it is that it was quite difficult, at times, to get much done. While they were all Arabs, there were many factions with different interpretations of the Holy Book, the Koran.

And they were quite anxious to mount a horse, take sword in hand, and emphasize their belief, and impose it upon others!

His information included the fact that Marrakesh is surrounded by a palm grove of about 32,000 acres. The city has two sections—The European and the Arab, (Medina.)

Aside from all the Mosques, he stressed visiting the Place El Djemaa, the Souks, the Mamounia Gardens the Agdal, an imperial gate, and the surrounding red walls. It seemed like quite a list—We wondered how long it would take to accomplish all that!

Before he was able to continue he was called to the phone. When he returned a few minutes later he said that events at the office required his attention. We said our good-byes, shook hands, and wished each other good luck. If we were going to stay in Marrakesh he would have made an invaluable friend. I can not say that we helped him very much.

That afternoon we drove around Marrakesh. The Koutoubia was visible from almost everywhere. It was built in the 12th century. It stands some 200 feet high with three golden balls at the top. Legend tells us that the balls were made form a Sultans jewels.

One story says that the jewels belonged to the Sultans wife. The Koutoubia walls are of carved stone. Inside there are six rooms, one on top of the other. It is a most impressive monument. The appearance, the color of the tower, varies with the light.

Marrakech is surrounded by red mud walls. Well, that depends upon the lighting. We were there more than a week—The color of the walls varies with the time of day, the intensity and direction of the sun light.—And, I guess the attitude of the viewer. It deserves its name—The rose city.

During our wanderings we ran upon the Mamounia Gardens. They are several centuries old and contain many orange, tangerine, and lemon trees. The gardens and the Hotel were lavish and inviting. Since we had made it that far we decided to try for a look inside. It was ornate! And it was exclusive—I had the same feeling that I did when we arrived in front of the Casino in Monaco on our 150 BSA motorcycle with all our camping gear aboard. We made our way to the gift shop—Well, it is not really a gift shop! Not only did I not see anything that I might ever want or use—I did not see anything that I could ever afford to

Buy! Although no one said anything, I felt so out of place that I suggested we make for the camper and the public road before we were placed in a Marrakesh Jail on a vagrancy charge!

After we left we got talking about Winston Churchill. He enjoyed spending vacations in Marrakesh. He loved to paint and he could never run out of subjects in, and around, Marrakesh.

One evening, just about dusk, we came upon a beautiful garden surrounding a large pool of water. It could have been the Menara Gardens. The large pool reflected a pavilion. We were hungry—We decided to eat. Emma got everything ready, had the table set, and the food on the plates. Suddenly, the rocks started to hit the camper. We had no idea where they might be coming from—It was dark, not possible to ascertain whether it was adults or children. Emma thinks she saw several young men. When the table was down it was not possible for me to reach the door. The table had to be cleared. There was pandemonium until I was able to get outside. We looked for the culprits first on foot and then with the camper—We tried using the headlights—No one was to be seen.

The incident was reported to the police. They tried to be helpful but what could they really do? No serious damage was done—Except to our nervous systems—and, several permanent dents in the old VW! We had never had such an incident in Morocco—We were more disappointed than we were upset. It turned out to be a good thing—After that we were much more careful about where we parked. But, we
Did not allow it to dampen our spirits or our determination to continue on our way.

From Rabat we drove along the coast road toward Casa. The surface was very good the view excellent, so we were able to cruise at the breath-taking speed of 40 MPH! We skirted the edge of Casa., headed south through Settat. We went through Mechra-Benabbou, and to a view-point south of Sidi-Bou-Othmane. The views south of Sidi-Bou-Othman of the Atlas Mountains were spectacular! We approached Marrakesh through a Palm Grove—Could not find a campsite that suited us and ended up camped near the air port! Not a quiet site but, we were so tired that it did not matter.

I would like to make a brief comment about Arab names. In school French and German, and music, were difficult for me. Fortunately I did not have to take Arabic—But, I have been sorry that it was not possible for me to try.

The next morning we had to head for the bank and the American Express. Even though our expenditures were minimal, food and fuel had to be paid for in dinars.

There was no problem at the bank. U.S. currency was quite welcome! The amount that we had to exchange was not impressive. We made our way to the American Express Office.

Our business at the American Express was handled by a middle-aged man who spoke French—But, not to us! He was very helpful and when we were finished he said that
He was very busy at the moment but he would have time to meet us at the hotel nearby the following morning. We readily accepted.

We were waiting when he arrived at the sidewalk café next morning. He went over a list of several things in Marrakesh that should not be missed.

# SQUARE JEMAA EL FNA

It was much more interesting than our guidebook. He stressed seeing the Square Je maa El Fna. That, he said was the one most important thing to see in Marrakech! Later, after visiting the Square several times, we agreed that he was absolutely right. To visit Marrakesh and not see the Square would have to be rated as a major blunder! Just as interesting was the information that he had lived in Marrakesh for many years. He was there when independence was gained in 1956. He told us that freedom was granted to the Moroccans at a high price. He touched on the fact that there are many factions in the country and that a unified front was not easy to form—Or to maintain. He said that he was married to an Arab woman. They had no children. Emma asked him if he ever considered leaving Morocco—"Never! He said he would never think of leaving Marrakech! "They would have to order us out."

Then it was his turn to ask questions—What did we do in the States? How could we travel for ten months? Where did we plan to go? What would we do upon our return? But, it did not seem like an interrogation. There was nothing to hide on our part. We had no way of knowing who he really was but we were very open as to our background. It was possible that two suspicious characters like us wandering about in a foreign country would arouse curiosity. It was a pleasure to talk with him—But it was not to last. The phone rang, he was needed back at the office. We said our goodbyes and parted company.

When you travel you meet so many people like that. All types of people, and as the years go by you wonder what has happened to them. At that moment in time we could not be too concerned about that. We had to find the Municipal Campground, eat, and be ready to see the sights in and around Marrakesh. We found the campground to be quite spacious—Some grass and many trees for welcome shade. Each camper selected his own site. There were many VW Campers scattered all over the area. There were lots of vehicles from all over Europe and we do not know how many motor bikes and motor cycles—And bicycles! One vehicle caught our attention at once. It was an armored car, the type Used by Brinks. Several Germans were traveling in it, One spoke English. They had intended to drive out into the Sahara from Goulimene in the south of Morocco! Obviously they were very naïve.

We had been down in Goulimene on a previous trip. Did they know that the road turned into a sand track with very difficult, hard to detect, soft spots? No. Had they calculated the amount of fuel that would be required? No. Did they have the required spare parts? No. Any provisions for food and water if they got stranded? No. Did they have the necessary sand-tracks for that heavy vehicle? Any spare tires? No.

Well, they were as prepared for a Saharan Adventure as an Englishman and a crazy American that we had encountered in Morocco. Those two adventurers had an
American Jeep with four-wheel drive—And absolutely nothing else! They were also headed for Goulimene. One day I told them that sometimes chicken wire can be used in place of sand tracks. The next day they showed up with a huge roll of chicken wire on top of the Jeep! I told the Englishman that their expedition was one of the least prepared that we had ever seen!

Fortunately we knew that when they arrived in Goulimene they would be stopped by the police. Still, some such "expeditions" slip past and a search party has to go out and find them. Unfortunately, the search party does not always arrive in time!

Of course there were hippies in ample supply. They sat in the back of their Vws and smoked pot. We never found out where the money came from. We think it was sent from home. The hippies were there "to find themselves." We can not report one case of success. Emma said that, in years to come they will find themselves without any education or specialty. We did wonder what ever happened to the hippies.

We can report one case of failure. A pretty young girl arrived one evening and she was crying! She related all her problems to Emma. She wanted to Part Company with her Hippy friends and go home—But, she had no money! Was it a ploy, a con game, or was it the truth? Emma is such an easy mark. She wanted to help her—So did I. However, we had a very long way to go, we did not know what might happen—And we had to be careful that we did not run out of money! Emma worried about her for days. So did I. She never returned to our camper. That made me suspicious. We sincerely hope she got out of the mess she was in. Another case—We will never know—

There were interesting plants and insects all over the camp. However, the ablution block was one of my favorites! Every morning and evening the most attractive German and French girls appeared there—And, so did I! Everything had to be done in the open air. After considerable close observation and contemplation, I came to the conclusion that everything was being done in the proper manner!

After a few days of much-needed rest—And after thoroughly cleaning the camper inside and out—We decided to make a tour along the mud-walls toward the famous Square Djemaa El Fna.

Merchants were setting up shop for the day. Some with old pickup trucks, some with donkeys with and without carts, and some carrying their wares on their backs! They did not have time to appreciate the beautiful sun rise or the play of light on the walls. As the sun rises the display of light changes from pink to red.

We were not pleased about getting up early—But, after seeing the display of light on the walls and the vendors, we changed out attitude. I have to Say, "If you have the money, and the time, you must visit Morocco and Marrakech!"

After some wandering around we located the Square. The problem then was how to find a safe place to park. Left alone, the camper would certainly be a target. Some distance from the Square there was a center, several main avenues converged. We pulled into a parking place. A young man approached us, he was able to speak as much English as we could speak Arabic! By pointing to the eyes and the vehicle it was obvious that he wanted to guard the camper. He was quite small, thin, and just about ragged. We could not turn down his offer. We had to take the chance.

The sun was still very low in the sky when we arrived at the Square. It was probably about a half mile away. Red to pink light played along the beautifully and intricately carved walls of the Koutoubia Tower. The little wooden stalls began to open as the merchants prepared for the days business.

History tells us that the square has an interesting past. I do not think that I would want to have been there. A governor had the habit of displaying, on posts, the heads of "criminals" executed the previous week! We can only hope that some of the dissidents were deported.

However, there is one record of Marrakesh being invaded by a religious sect—The entire population of the native people of a different sect were exterminated! That was one way of controlling the population!

As the stalls opened and the water was boiled for mint tea, traveling merchants, carrying their loads on their backs or on burrows, set up shop all around the square. Each shop was specialized. Some sold soup, others offered biscuits, cookies, bread, and a variety of things that, either I can not remember or could not identify! As the sun rose the Square came to life! Throughout the morning the activity intensified. But, there were brief periods of calm. Even the haggling of the merchants with potential customers over the prices became quiet!

Five times a day everything stopped! The call to prayer by the Muezzin came blaring over loudspeakers, it could be heard everywhere. Some people faced Mecca and said their prayers where they were. Others seem to have left for the nearest Mosque. Anyway, in a very short time, all former activity was resumed.

We went into a café on the square for tea. It was served on the roof giving us a panoramic view. It was a very pleasant break. The tea was served in typical Arab style—The waiter poured it into the small glass from a height that seemed very dangerous! There seemed to be the real possibility that I might get scalded. That did not happen. From our vantage point I tried to get some pictures of the constantly changing activity all over the huge four-acre square. Emma was acting as my spotter—We must have made quite a scene. The fact that someone might be listening, and understanding, everything we said did not occur to us. Fortunately we were so fascinated by the scene that it never occurred to us to be critical in any way. That scene has been played out for hundreds of years!

When we finished and sat down with our tea a man dressed in Arab clothes—Red Fez hat and long woven burnoose, approached the table and ask if he might join us. He spoke English and we were delighted to be able to talk to someone.

He wanted to know the usual information—Where? Going to? Traveling by how long in Morocco? We did not mind his curiosity, it seemed natural. He was living in Marrakesh, had two wives, and had some kind of government position. He seemed to want to talk about the political situation in Morocco. We had learned the hard way years past that it is best to be very careful about what one says in that area.

He did the talking and we listened. We knew almost nothing about the political situation. We did know that Morocco was trying to unify and become independent since about 1912. He related that France and Germany almost started the First World War at about that time. While it was interesting and informative, it was really not our area of Interest. What was of interest, and news to us, was that, even though Morocco gained its independence in 1956, it was far from unified. The Berber Tribes in the mountains remain fiercely independent they want the Berber language taught in the schools. The desert tribes, at times, put on rather violent demonstrations. He said, Morocco is not as unified as many people abroad think—The King has powerful enemies and they must be carefully watched." Some of the dissidents are "deported" to the south—The area in, and around, Goulimine.

His advice was to be careful about getting involved with any group or faction. On a previous visit to Morocco we had been caught in some kind of violent protest. The unruly crowd surrounded the camper and, although we had no connection or idea of what was happening, it was potentially dangerous. Fortunately troops appeared. They were well trained and did not hesitate to use their long night sticks very Effectively. The angry mob melted away—At least for the moment. And we lost no time getting out of the village.

After we told him about the incident he said such protests are quite common. The wise thing is to try to foresee them and head in another direction! Depending upon the current news, it might be wise to avoid places where Americans tend to congregate!

The sun was getting higher in the sky. It was getting very hot out on that roof! We were hot and hungry. We could not understand how he was able to appear so cool in that heavy robe! We thanked him for his information and his time. (He seemed to have plenty of both!) Activity in the square had slowed down noticeably. We decided that if they were going to take a break we would return to the camper for lunch. The food looked and smelled very good but Emma thought it best not to take any unnecessary chances. We did not want to get sick—Why take the risk? That was another advantage of the camper—Being able to cook our own food. Not an easy feat on a one-burner gas stove! But, Emma managed it just about three times a day—And never complained! I was very fortunate to have such a wonderful traveling buddy!

When we arrived back at the camp some Germans had arrived in a passenger bus pulling a large trailer. There were 36 passengers. People were everywhere all busy doing something . . . . The trailer in which they slept at night was long, and quite high. It had three rows of windows. Each window is a cubicle for sleeping they had folding tables and chairs at which they were writing letters and cards. Many were just resting in the sun. More than understandable, if you have been in Europe during the winter.

The Trailer had sleeping compartments—Each one about two feet square. How some of those portly Germans managed to get into, and out of, those elongated boxes I was never able to learn. Another problem—How does one survive a long hot night?

A small window opened to the outside at one end of each compartment!

A canvas covered a kitchen cooking facility at the rear of the trailer. At mealtime everyone lined up and received his meal. We do not think that any gourmet meals were served.

If you are living in Europe during the winter and you do not have much money—And you want to see some sunshine—And you are not demanding with respect to comfort—The journey to Marrakesh is well worth the hardship.

Emma and I were in no position to critize those people! We were happily living in a VW Camper. It was one of the first space capsules. Quite a few Europeans were doing the same—But, we saw very few Americans!

One other American couple did arrive at the camp in a VW camper. They were very quiet—kept strictly to themselves. We never saw them at the ablution block, they never seemed to cook in the campground. We were more curious about them than anyone else! All out questions remained unanswered. Very frustrating.

Between visits to the Square it was necessary to clean the VW. Emma took care of the inside, with all the sand and dust it amounted to a redistribution process. It did help—Well, it made us feel better. While that was taking place it fell upon me to do something about the outside of the vehicle. We carried a bucket and sponges and cloths for just such a purpose. I seem to remember Emma mentioning the sand and dirt on the camper several times. Actually, it did not keep me awake at night. Anyway, one day, I finally got it done. The old contraption did look a little more presentable.

From the campground, and from the city, we had wonderful views of the snow-capped Atlas Mountains. Michael Palin, in his book, "Sahara" mentions that he never saw such views. (2000) we think that the reason is the development that has taken place—And, the tremendous increase in the population!!

The days passed quickly in Marrakesh. The air seemed fresh and clear, the view of the mountains varied by the hour, by the minute! We were able to drive into town for tea, or for a meal. Shopping could be done in the souk or in modern grocery stores in the European quarter. There were many escorted trips to various areas all around. In the evening Musicians dance and play drums they had tassel on their hats that twirled around as they danced.

It was time for us to visit the Square during the evening. Business is transacted during the morning—The atmosphere changes late in the afternoon. We ate early one afternoon and went into the European section where we usually parked. Our boy guard appeared out of thin air! Did he live there or did he have a hiding place? No matter—He was very willing to guard the camper—And by that time we had every confidence in him. Every time we paid him it involved candy bars and four or five dirhams. He appeared to be very satisfied. We always wondered about his family life—If he had one!

We were told that he may have been working for a boss of some type. He may not have been able to keep what he earned. That is also supposed to be true with respect to the numerous beggars. As a tourist it is impossible to learn what is really going on behind what is seen. It seems to be a serious mistake to draw conclusions with respect to a society by a short trip. We were not there to judge the Moroccan society!

Once again we found ourselves having tea and peering down on the frantic scene laid out below us. We had a spectacular panorama. As the light faded little lights came into view all over, and around the Square! Best not to over-use the word spectacular!!

Some of the stalls were closing, some were lighting lamps and lanterns in hopes of one more customer. The last rays of the sun played out on the Koutoubia Tower. The story-teller had gathered and even larger, and more attentive, audience. It would have been fascinating to have been able to understand what he was saying. The dim light of a lantern played over his wrinkled face—He had very impressive gestures and an ever-changing expression. We had seen him close up earlier in the day. It would have been the ideal setting in which to tell ancient ghost or murder stories. We wondered if that was his subject. Again—We would never know.

The dancers from Mauritania were still going strong. Chanting and dancing in a circle, dressed in white, tossing the tassels at the tops of their turbans. They were worth more than the few dirhams collected when they passed through the crowd

As we looked over the scene unfolding before us the subject of ethnicity came up. Emma said it certainly looks like a well-integrated society. From our vantage point it certainly did appear that way. But, the people of Morocco are a mixture of many nationalities. There have been many different religious sects as I have mentioned. Unfortunately that has resulted in considerable blood-shed. It can only be hoped that the present population will be able to resolve their different interpretations of the Koran in more peaceful ways. And, Emma said, that applies to us as well.

While we were on that serious and historical note the subject of genes came up. History indicates that the Berbers once dominated all across North Africa. The first settlements were Phoenician, then came the Romans, followed briefly by the Vandals, then the Europeans.

Each of those groups contributed genes to the existing population. It has been quite a mixture! While many of the Berber Tribes kept to themselves, there has been considerable cross-breeding. That would best be taken up by anthropologists and genetics—It is fascinating, we thought, but far beyond our comprehension.

The day had faded into evening and then night! The noise-level subsided, the crowd began to disappear into the darkness, and the little lights started to go out. It was time for us to find our way out!

Everything looked quite unfamiliar in the relative darkness! We could not ask anyone for directions. We were not afraid—But, we were on our own. Emma was quite well oriented—At least better oriented than I was! She knew that we had to head east—Good news—But which way was east? There is a rather large intersection at the entrance to the Square—We walked until we found that—Then we knew where we were. There was light—Some light—At no time did we feel that we were in danger. But, we were very relieved to see the camper—And our faithful boy-guard!

He probably could not understand what happened—But, he certainly was pleased to get three candy bars and eight dirhams! We were so happy to find our way out and to see the camper undamaged that we thought he was well worth what he was paid. He had earned it! Then, it was back to the campground—And directly into bed! We had to check the maps and plan our exit from Marrakesh. That was something that we were not really anxious to do. The rough plan was to head for Figuig by way of Zagora.

That route would take us over the Tizi-n-Tichka Pass, through Ouarzazate, and down the Vallee du Dra, into Zagora. From Zagora it would be necessary to return to Ouarzazate., go through the dades Valley, Tinerhir and the Gorges du Todra. Then to Ksar-es-Souk, Boudenib, and east to the Oasis of Figuig on the border of Algeria and into the real Sahara—At last!

# MARRAKESH
# TO FIGUIG

Before Leaving Marrakech, last minute preparations needed to be made. Emma had to shop for food that would not spoil on the road. The VW did not have refrigeration—That added to Emma's problems. However, it was possible to buy fresh fruit and vegetables in the markets in every village. Just another problem that she managed to work around.

My responsibility was the maintenance of the VW. That involved checking the oil in the motor and transmission. The air filter had to be cleaned and fresh oil added. Fortunately a paper filter was not required. The filter was cleaned with gasoline, then covered with motor oil. It was not something I looked forward to—But it worked very well. Setting the valves was a constant chore—They required setting every 2500 miles. The motor had to be cold. Adjusting the distributor points did not take much time. The fan belt was important—It operated the cooling fan—The motor would burn up without it!

The gasoline cans had to be topped off and extra oil stored. The tires were new just needed the air pressure set. We carried tools required for general maintenance—But, a major breakdown could create a very serious situation. People have driven out into the Sahara without due notice to the Perfect (Police Chief.) If the police do not know that you have left, they can not search for you! Unfortunately that has resulted in rather frequent fatalities!

Although we were not yet in the Sahara, we were entering the edge of it. We were in the foothills of the Atlas Mountains—Help was still readily available. If you do break down, other travelers will offer all the help that they can. In the desert you must stop and Offer assistance!

On our way out of Marrakesh there was one last thing to do. We had to stop at our usual parking place off the Square and see if our boy guard might be there—He was! He was happy to see us but he knew that we were leaving. It was not necessary to tell him. The usual candy and dirhams were gratefully accepted. Still, we all were sad. We, and he, knew that we would never meet again. As I have mentioned, that is often the down-side of traveling—It is part of the experience.

It was quiet in the camper as we exited Marrakesh. There were so many things to think about. Uppermost in our minds was the Great Square—And all the different people who made it unique. Not unique just in Morocco—Unique in the world!

The palm groves, the Mosques, the gardens, the location on the vast plain, the multi-colored walls, the souks, the sun rising and setting, they all fade when you think of standing along the second-floor restaurant wall and drinking your tea while looking down on the never-ending spectacle of life unfolding before your eyes!

# BERBERS IN
# THE ATLAS MOUNTAINS

The paved road took us east and then south, past Ait-Qurir and toward the Tizi-n-Tichka Pass. The warnings about the steep grade and the switch-backs were very much on my mind. I knew that the camper was over-loaded. There was no way to lighten the load and be prepared for safe travel through the Sahara.

Beyond Ait-Barka the road starts to twist and turn. The pass is well over 6000 feet high. We were in the High Atlas Mountains! That would be a good test for the old VW! It was! During the climb

During the climb I went up and down through the gears. While the vehicle did not have much horsepower, it did have reduction gears on both rear drive wheels. When you got down into first gear it would climb up the walls. (Well maybe not quite that good!) On one sharp turn we met a tour bus. That required considerable maneuvering on his part and on mine. The VW was smaller and much easier to jockey back and forth. We both continued on our way.

The tourists are transported from Marrakesh over the pass and down to Zagora. They call it the Big South and Kasbahs tour. It is that. But, such tours moved much too fast for us! A lot of packing and unpacking is required. Then, there Thing. But, the scenery is worth much more than the inconvenience.

It was getting late when we reached the top of the pass. There were patches of snow on the ground—Nothing to worry about—We often camped in the snow. A grove of Hugh Cypress trees provided an ideal camp spot for the night. Sight-seeing takes a lot of energy! To take pictures it is necessary to climb into and out of the camper—Not the easiest thing to do frequently.

After the sun set it became quite chilly. Our heating system consisted of a small propane heater—It was better than no heater at all! Using the battery for light could, over the course of a long evening, drain the battery. The VW did not have separate "house" batteries. The answer? Put on our "long-johns" and go to bed!

In the morning (early!!) We heard sounds of people, sheep, goats, donkeys, and camels! It did not take long to discover the source of the sound—A Berber Market was in full swing a short distance away. The line of little white tents were up and the selling, bargaining, and browsing was taking place. Hot mint tea was ready to be served. Also big metal pots of stew were cooking—And the aroma was drawing a large clientele.

The setting was spectacular!! I might have used "beautiful" but I have used both those words all the way across Morocco. You must excuse me—As you must know by now, my vocabulary is rather limited. You must just try to imagine those Berbers, in their turbans and heavy wool, expertly woven burnooses, all going about their business, in, and around, their white neat tents

The whole scene taking place in the brisk Mountain air under those beautiful Cypress trees.

Emma and I joined the browser a great variety of local and imported products were available. Emma bought some sugar, salt, goat milk, and some hand-woven place-mats. We still have them! If you were a Berber and they did not have what you wanted—You did not need it!

All kinds of animals were being sold and traded—Sheep, goats donkeys, camels. We looked them all over and decided that, while we would like very much to have one or two of each at home—We had best stick with the VW for the rest of this trip.

The Berber tribes in the Atlas Mountains are very interesting. They have been there for thousands of years—And, there is every indication that some of them will be there for some time into the future. They were there before the Phoenicians arrived several thousand years ago. The Phoenicians were great traders. They set up trading posts all along the North African coast. The Berbers traded with them but did not really accept them or their culture. History indicates that the Phoenicians were not interested in territory—They were business people. They sailed along the North African coast, through the Straits of Gibraltar, and down the West Coast of what is now Morocco. Phoenician coins have been found along the African Coast down to ports in Mauritania, Guinea, and Cameron. There does not seem to be any creditable evidence that they made it all the way around the continent of Africa.

After the Phoenicians came the Carthaginians. Their empire extended farther inland—When they were defeated by the Romans there was a period of peace and relative prosperity that lasted several hundred years. They built cities and fortifications deep into the Sahara. But, of course, they too faded from history. Then there was the Vandal invasion—Finally, to complete this brief historical record—In the seventh and eighth centuries the Arab invaders swept across North Africa. The most recent invasion came from Europe—The European powers took it upon themselves to save and educate all the Africans! We know how that Grand Idea turned out.

And now the people of North Africa are left to sort out the mess that they have been left. It is going to take a long time! In addition to all that they have a very serious population crisis! If they fail to solve that one, the problems will not matter.

When I got off the track back there—I was trying to point out that the Berbers as a people lived through all the invasions—And pretty much with their basic culture in tact. At present they seem to have accepted the Moslem Religion—And from what we could observe as tourists passing through, not much else.

The Berbers have always had to deal with incursions from the desert tribes. There seems to have been a constant see-saw battle between the nomad herders and the settled farmers. The farmers have been driven back into the mountains for safety. They have built kasbahs and fortified villages and granaries. They have proven to be resourceful and adaptable. They seem to be able to adjust to changing circumstances and maintain their cultural traditions.

The day was spent wandering about in the market. We got hungry but did not want to miss anything—So we each had a bowl of stew. It was really good! I have no idea what was in it!

It seemed to us that everything in the market was for sale or trade. Before a sale could be concluded there was an almost endless round of discussion and hand waving. At the end they seemed to shake hands and put one hand over their hearts. We really had no idea of what was taking place—But we had a great time as observers. The people were very friendly, they smiled easily, offered us places to sit down and rest—and, of course, tried to sell us things that we could not identify—Or ever use.

I said they smiled easily—Both men and women. The women do not wear veils. They are more free in public, and in private, than typical Arab women. We were told that although the women are more free, they still are considered inferior to the men. Well, not being able to understand their dialect or live with them, we will just have to accept that as fact!

When we got up the next morning they were gone! Nothing was left. There was a large crowd there! Nothing was left to be cleaned up! Emma said what I was thinking—Could such a thing ever happen in the United States!!

We often discuss that experience. It was not planned—We had no idea when we went to bed that we would be able to visit a Berber Market in the Atlas Mountains when we got up!

Did we talk about being able to live in the Atlas Mountains with the Berbers—Indeed we did! But, our culture is so different—It could be done by some people—We just wondered if we would be able to make such a transition??

Well, we had to shift gears and move on—The winter weather would not last forever. Spring, and hot weather arrives very early in the Sahara—We traveled so slowly—We were to learn about the heat in the Sahara the hard way! Experience taught us that it would have been much wiser to allow ten months for Morocco—And a full winter in the Sahara. (Yes! Ten months for Morocco!!)

The tourists were not our problem. Our objective was to make it to Ouarzazate. The town was started by the French as an administrative center—It was also a military outpost. It is now a relatively large city. A major stop for the tour busses and people like us. Emma bought some fresh food and we filled the fuel tank. Best to keep it full even though there was plenty available in that area. The town was well-kept—It was more of a tourist center—Not really of great interest to us. Up to that point the best part of the trip was the Tizi-n-Tichka Pass.

South of Ouarzazate the scenery really improved. We were traveling through foot-hills of the Atlas—Where it starts to blend into the Sahara—But, you are not there yet!

Through the Jbel Sahara the road makes some sharp twists and turns. From the village of Agdz south there is one beautiful view after another. The mountain views and the mud-walled Ksars or Bordjs are spectacular! We were told that it is often used as the setting for movies.

South of Agdz we started to pass through very attractive Ksars, and then the Palm Groves came into view. The road follows theVallee du Dra into Zagora. Now we were on the edge of the Great Sahara! That is as far as most tourists are able to travel. We thought about how fortunate we were to be able to travel and see what we had already seen while crossing Morocco.

The great scenery! The fascinating variety of people! How exciting to be able to see all the sights and listen to the variety of sounds! This is, indeed, a perfect planet! We thought about how lucky we were!

But—There is always a but—There was a dark side. There are some very rich people in Morocco and they have no intention of sharing with the have-nots. There are just too many people in Morocco

Of course there are far too many of us on the planet! That situation creates fertile breeding ground for very serious problems. The problem exists all over the planet. It is much easier to see it than it is to begin to fix it. Every country that we have ever visited faces the same situation!

A rather weighty discussion to be carried out in an old VW camper as it chugs its way down the beautiful Dra Valley.

Farther down the valley the palm trees slowly thin out as the river becomes smaller and finally disappears into the sands of the Sahara. Also, the multi-storied mud-brick fortified ksars also disappear. The mud-walled homes are very picturesque from the outside, set along the valley on the hills and with the mountains as background. However, many people would find daily life something of a hardship if they were required to adapt to such conditions. More about this later.

From Ouarzazate down along the valley into Zagora one beautiful scene blends into another! I know that I am over-working the word "beautiful"—I must try to change that!

The Ksars have not been built on fertile land—That is devoted entirely to raising food and other crops. In America and China prime land is devoted to industry and housing. Industry and large tracts of homes apparently make more money. When the population-food crises is upon the people they must intend to eat money in order to live!

Beyond the gate you enter a huge open square! Along one side a line of arched, covered shops, open facing the square. The variety of goods available is surprising! As they say—If they do not have it—You do not need it! The merchants work hard for the money they make. But, that does not mean that you should not bargain.

Before Leaving Marrakech, last minute preparations needed to be made. Emma had to shop for food that would not spoil on the road. The VW did not have refrigeration—That added to Emma's problems. However, it was possible to buy fresh fruit and vegetables in every village. Just another problem that she managed to work around.

My responsibility was the maintenance of the VW. That involved checking the oil in the motor and transmission. The air filter had to be cleaned and fresh oil added. Fortunately a paper filter was not required. The filter was cleaned with gasoline, then covered with motor oil. It was not something I looked forward to—But it worked very well. Setting the valves was a constant chore—They required setting every 2500 miles. The motor had to be cold. Adjusting the distributor points did not take much time. The fan belt was important—It operated the cooling fan—The motor would burn up without it!

The gasoline cans had to be topped off and extra oil stored. The tires were new, just needed the air pressure set. We carried tools required for general maintenance—But, a major breakdown could create a very serious situation. People have driven out into the Sahara without due notice to the Perfect (Police Chief). If the police do not know that you have left, they can not search for you! Unfortunately that has resulted in rather frequent fatalities!

Although we were not yet in the Sahara, we were entering the edge of it. We were in the foothills of the Atlas Mountains—Help was still readily available. If you do break down, other travelers will offer all the help that they can. In the desert you must stop and Offer assistance!

On our way out of Marrakesh there was one last thing to do. We had to stop at our usual parking place off the Square and see if our boy guard might be there—He was! He was happy to see us but he knew that we were leaving. It was not necessary to tell him. The usual candy and dirhams were gratefully accepted. Still, we all were sad. We, and he, knew that we would never meet again. As I have mentioned, that is often the down-side of traveling—It is part of the experience.

It was quiet in the camper as we exited Marrakesh. There were so many things to think about. Uppermost in our minds was the Great Square—And all the different people who made it unique. Not unique just in Morocco—Unique in the world!

The palm groves, the Mosques, the gardens, the location on the vast plain, the multi-colored walls, the souks, the sun rising and setting, they all fade when you think of standing along the second-floor restaurant wall and drinking your tea while looking down on the never-ending spectacle of life unfolding before your eyes!

The paved road took us east and then south, past Ait-Qurir and toward the Tizi-n-Tichka Pass. The warnings about the steep grade and the switch-backs were very much on my mind. I knew that the camper was over-loaded. There was no way to lighten the load and be prepared for safe travel through the Sahara.

Beyond Ait-Barka the road starts to twist and turn. The pass is well over 6000 feet high. We were in the High Atlas Mountains! That would be a good test for the old VW! It was! During the climb I went up and down through the gears. While the vehicle did not have much horsepower, it did have reduction gears on both rear drive wheels. When you got down into first gear it would climb up the walls. (Well maybe not quite that good!) On one sharp turn we met a tour bus. That required considerable maneuvering on his part and on mine. The VW was smaller and much easier to jockey back and forth. We both continued on our way.

The tourists are transported from Marrakesh over the pass and down to Zagora. They call it the Big South and Kasbahs tour. It is that. But, such tours moved much too fast for us! A lot of packing and unpacking is required. Then, there are all those people at every stop—All trying to see, and photograph the same thing. But, the scenery is worth much more than the unconvinced.

It was getting late when we reached the top of the pass. There were patches of snow on the ground—Nothing to worry about—We often camped in the snow. A grove of Hugh Cypress trees provided an ideal camp spot for the night. Sight-seeing takes a lot of energy! To take pictures it is necessary to climb into and out of the camper—Not the easiest thing to do frequently.

After the sun set it became quite chilly. Our heating system consisted of a small propane heater—It was better than no heater at all! Using the battery for light could, over the course of a long evening, drain the battery.

The VW did not have separate "house" batteries. The answer Put on our "long-johns" and go to bed!

In the morning (early!!!) We heard sounds of people, sheep, goats, donkeys, and camels! It did not take long to discover the source of the sound—A Berber Market was in full swing a short distance away. The line of little white tents were up and the selling, bargaining, and browsing was taking place. Hot mint tea was ready to be served. Also big metal pots of stew were cooking—And the aroma was drawing a large clientele.

The setting was spectacular!! I might have used "beautiful" but I have used both those words all the way across Morocco. You must excuse me—As you must know by now, my vocabulary is rather limited. You must just try to imagine those Berbers, in their turbans and heavy wool, expertly woven burnooses, all going about their business, in, and around, their white neat tents

The whole scene taking place in the brisk mountain air under those beautiful Cypress trees. (There is that word again!)

Emma and I joined the browsers. A great variety of local, and imported products were available. Emma bought some sugar, salt, goat milk, and some hand-woven place-mats. We still have them! If you were a Berber and they did not have what you wanted—You did not need it!

All kinds of animals were being sold and traded—Sheep, goats. Donkeys, camels. We looked them all over and decided that, while we would like very much to have one or two of each at home—We had best stick with the VW for the rest of this trip.

The Berber tribes in the Atlas Mountains are very interesting. They have been there for thousands of years—And, there is every indication that some of them will be there for some time into the future. They were there before the Phoenicians arrived several thousand years ago. The Phoenicians were great traders. They set up trading posts all along the North African coast. The Berbers traded with them but did not really accept them or their culture. History indicates that the Phoenicians were not interested in territory—They were business people. They sailed along the North

African coast, through the Straits of Gibraltar, and down the West Coast of what is now Morocco. Phoenician coins have been found along the African Coast down to ports in Mauritania, Guinea, and Cameron. There does not seem to be any creditable evidence that they made in all the way around the continent of Africa.

After the Phoenicians came the Carthaginians. Their empire extended farther inland—When they were defeated by the Romans there was a period of peace and relative prosperity that lasted several hundred years. They built cities and fortifications deep into the Sahara. But, of course, they too faded from history. Then there was the Vandal invasion—Finally, to complete this brief historical record—In the seventh and eighth centuries the Arab invaders swept across North Africa. The most recent invasion came from Europe—The European powers took it upon themselves to save and educate all the Africans!! We know how that Grand Idea turned out.

And now the people of North Africa are left to sort out the mess that they have been left. It is going to take a long time! In addition to all that they have a very serious population crisis! If they fail to solve that one the problems will not matter.

When I got off the track back there—I was trying to point out that the Berbers as a people lived through all the invasions—And pretty much with their basic culture in tact. At present they seem to have accepted the Moslem Religion—And from what we could observe as tourists passing through, not much else.

The Berbers have always had to deal with incursions from the desert tribes. There seems to have been a constant see-saw battle between the nomad herders and the settled farmers. The farmers have been driven back into the mountains for safety. They have built kasbahs and fortified villages and granaries. They have proven to be resourceful and adaptable. They seem to be able to adjust to changing circumstances and maintain their cultural traditions.

The day was spent wandering about in the market. We got hungry but did not want to miss anything—So we each had a bowl of stew. It was really good! I have no idea what was in it!

It seemed to us that everything in the market was for sale or trade. Before a sale could be concluded there was an almost endless round of discussion and hand waving. At the end they seemed to shake hands and put one hand over their hearts. We really had no idea of what was taking place—But we had a great time as observers.

The people were very friendly, they smiled easily, offered us places to sit down and rest—And, of course, tried to sell us things that we could not identify—Or ever use.

I said they smiled easily—Both men and women. The women do not wear veils. They are more free in public, and in private, than typical Arab women. We were told that although the women have more freedom, they still are considered inferior to the men. Well, not being able to understand their dialect or live with them, we will just have to accept that as fact!

When we got up the next morning they were gone! Nothing was left. There was a large crowd there! Nothing was left to be cleaned up, we did not think that could happen in the States!!

We often discuss that experience. It was not planned—We had no idea when we went to bed that we would be able to visit a Berber Market in the Atlas Mountains when we got up!

Did we talk about being able to live in the Atlas Mountains with the Berbers—Indeed we did! But, our culture is so different—It could be done by some people—We just wondered if we would be able to make such a transition??

Well, we had to shift gears and move on—The winter weather would not last forever. Spring, and hot weather arrives very early in the Sahara—We traveled so slowly—We were to learn about the heat in the Sahara the hard way! Experience taught us that it would have been much wiser to allow ten months for Morocco—And a full winter in the Sahara. (Yes Ten months for Morocco!!)

The tourists were not our problem. Our objective was to make it to Ouarzazate. The town was started by the French as an administrative center—It was also a military outpost. It is now a relatively large city. A major stop for the tour busses and people like us. Emma bought some fresh food and we filled the fuel tank. Best to keep it full even though there was plenty available in that area. The town was well-kept—It was more of a tourist center—Not really of great interest to us. Up to that point the best part of the trip was the Tizi-n-Tichka Pass.

South of Ouarzazate the scenery really improved. We were traveling through foot-hills of the Atlas—Where it starts to blend into the Sahara—But, you are not there yet!

# JBEL SAHARA

Through the Jbel Sahara the road makes some sharp twists and turns. From the village of Agdz south there is one beautiful view after another. The mountain views and the mud-walled Ksars or Bordjs are spectacular. We were told that it is often used as the setting for movies.

South of Agdz we started to pass through very attractive Ksars, and then the Palm Groves came into view. The road follows the Vallee du Dra into Zagora. Now we were on the edge of the Great Sahara! That is as far as most tourists are able to travel. We thought about how fortunate we were to be able to travel and see what we had already seen while crossing Morocco.

The great scenery! The fascinating variety of people! How exciting to be able to see all the sights and listen to the variety of sounds! This is, indeed, a perfect planet! We thought about how lucky we were!

But—There is always a but—There was a dark side. There are some very rich people in Morocco—And there are a great many very poor people. The haves have no intention of sharing with the have-nots. There are just too many people in Morocco. Of course there are far too many of us on the planet! That situation creates fertile breeding ground for very serious problems. The problem exists all over the planet. It is much easier to see it than it is to begin to fix it. Every country that we have ever visited faces the same situation! A rather weighty discussion to be carried out in an old VW camper as it chugs its way down the beautiful Dra Valley.

Farther down the valley the palm trees slowly thin out as the river becomes smaller and finally disappears into the sands of the Sahara. Also, the multi-storied mud-brick fortified ksars disappear.

The mud-walled homes are very picturesque from the outside, set along the valley on the hills and with the mountains as background. However, many people would find daily life something of a hardship if they were required to adapt to such conditions. More about this later.

From Ouarzazate down along the valley into Zagora one beautiful scene blends into another!

The Ksars have not been built on fertile land—That is devoted entirely to raising food and other crops. In America and China prime land is devoted to industry and housing. Industry and large tracts of homes apparently make more money. When the population-food crises is upon the people they must intend to eat money in order to live!

## *ZAGORA*

The entrance into Zagora is through a huge horseshoe—shaped arch. It is quite impressive! The main street is named Mohammed 1V—I think! That would be a safe guess for the name of the main street in any town in Morocco.

Beyond the gate you enter a huge open square! Along one side a line of arched, covered shops, open facing the square. The variety of goods available is surprising! As they say—If they do not have it—You do not need it! The merchants work hard for the money they make. But, that does not mean that you should make an
Offer that they can't refuse.

The merchants and traders are spread out all over the square. All kinds of people are trying to buy and sell. Sheep, goats, camels, carpets, locks, jewelry, even cameras! Everything has two prices—The asking price—And the selling price. If you do not know that it is your fault—Not the sellers!

Many people think of a parking lot as a place for cars—Not at the market in Zagora! There they have special pens in which you park your donkey, mule, horse, or camel. We were not able to find out the fee per hour, day, week, or whatever.

Of course there were several hotels in Zagora. There were several more under construction. Other so-called modern facilities were also available. They are essential to the tourist. They were of no interest to us. It is very understandable that people should want to see that area on the edge of the Sahara—And that they have to have all the comforts that they had at home.

The tour busses constantly disgorge hoards of overweight, camera—toting, over dressed and underdressed individuals who have no concept of where they are or what they are looking at. Many of them just can not wait until they get to the hotel for a drink and a shower. To many of them everything is most exciting! They want their picture taken in front of everything, and everybody. The poor little water-boy gets lots of hugs—Until the cameras snaps! It is far more interesting to watch his reaction, and that of the Merchants, than it is to watch the tourists. Well, just as interesting

By the way, the water-boy is well worth many pictures. The water is heavy, he walks all Over with it all day. He makes more posing for the tourist than he does selling water. It would be interesting to run an analysis of his water.

Frequent tours into the "desert" leave from Zagora. They probably do give the tourist some idea of the Sahara. However, a one—d ay tour, or a short flight can not really relate in ones brain the true vastness of the Sahara Desert!

Watching the tourists being herded onto and off the busses reminds one of life back in the States. Most people spend their entire working lives buying "things". Material things. They are so busy buying, and trying to pay for, their "things" that they have little or no time to appreciate what is all around them. Is that not a form of slavery??

Not many miles south of Zagora the road and the river just fade into the desert. If you plan to go on from here you had best have a land-rover! We did see one expedition leave. They were from Sweden and they had two land-rovers. One man told us that this was not their first venture into the Sahara.

The rovers looked like they could go anywhere. They were packed full of camping gear, with extra gas and water cans. They had two-way radios and two guides. We asked about what would happen to the guides when they ended their safari. "They will be paid and provided with two camels".

Emma and I rationalize—We justify our ten-month safaris by saying—Our ancestors were hunter-gathers, just as many of the tribes in and around the Sahara are today. The drive to explore what might be over the next hill is not in our blood—It is in our gene!

It was very obvious even before we saw the land-rovers that we were at the end of the road for the VW. Compared to their vehicles and provisions, we were really traveling on the knife-edge of a serious adventure. You have an adventure when something happens for which you are not prepared!

Back to Zagora and our "camp" just off the square. We were quite surprised—There were several beggars and many children all over the square. We did hand out candy and dinars to the extent that we thought we could afford. Anyway, when night fell everyone disappeared. We got into the camper, ate, made up the bed, and went to sleep. All kinds of stories circulate about the dangers of travel in this or that area—We can only speak about our own first-hand experience.

Several days were spent just wandering about the area of Zagora. Several authors write it off with a few sentences. They might be right. We found the people who lived there, and the constant visiting tribes' men and women from the surrounding desert really fascinating.

One morning we were awakened by music created by drums and flutes. Without breakfast we made a dash for the square. There, arranged in a circle were the drummers and flute-players. Each player took his turn in the center of the ring. They gyrated, jumped, and danced to the music. That performance, that atmosphere could not be recreated anywhere else! It had to be in the square in Zagora—The light, the dust, the wind carrying some sand in from the desert—That can never be re-created!

Could a writer, an artist, a photographer, a religious person, even a drop-out hippie, live there absolutely! And, I am sure, some do. (We do not remember seeing any Hippies—But, in a burnoose, who could tell?)

The night was spent a short distance from the market square—In the same place that we had used for several nights previously. Our strategy was to use the same spot since we had experienced no trouble there. The people certainly knew that we were camping in that area. The curtains were closed every night but we could peek out to see what was happening. Passers-by paid no attention to us.

In the morning we were awakened by the activity of the market. The vendors begin to arrive at dawn—They come in from their homes, the kasbahs, miles away. The pack animals have to be loaded long before the sun rises!

Once the activity starts it is necessary to get over to the square and observe the action, and there is plenty of it. The arched, covered stalls that open on one side toward the square are full of constant movement. The baskets and boxes of fruit, vegetables, and dates are put on display. The sellers are busy spreading their blankets and wares in the center of the square. The scene is one of constant and ever-changing action and color. As the sun begins to fill the square and reflect on the dust kicked up by the traders,

The water-boys wearing their colorful costumes constantly circulate through the melee. They wear wide-brimmed hats with tassels hanging from the rim. Their pants and vests are red and black. Each one carries a goat-skinned bag, a cup, and a small bell. Tourists were very few—But, if there were any, they would certainly want a picture of a water-boy. They did not ask us for money—But, we did pay a few dinars. I would not want to have to carry that bag of water around all day!

Emma made her way from stall to stall she used an exchange of verbal and sign language. Most people seem to expect the Arabs to try to cheat them—And, no doubt, many of them do. In Zagora we did not get that impression. During most transactions Emma just had to hold out the money and accept the change. She did know how many dinars we were getting on the dollar—So she was not really "flying blind."

It might be surprising but, I had no trouble finding motor oil. On second thought, there are many motor vehicles in use and all the spare parts, maintenance equipment, and skilled mechanics are necessary. Petrol was available so we filled the tanks—Same for water. As we got closer to the desert the distance between stations increased. If we did have any trouble the next lorry or truck would offer to help us.

Perhaps we are peculiar (some people are quite certain that we are) but we were reluctant to leave Zagora. Even if you can not speak their language, the people recognize that you are a guest in their country, they smile and wave and make you feel welcome. We try to keep in mind that we are guests in their country and behave accordingly.

After about a week in Zagora, our shopping was done and we knew that we had to head back up the Vallee du Dra toward Ouarzazate, turn right there and head east. That route would take us through Boumaine, Tinerhir and the Gorges du Todra, Ksar-es-Souk and the Gorges du Ziz. Then on east to Boudenib, Bouaria and Figuig on the Algerian border and the entrance to the Sahara Desert! The map indicates passes, ksars, rivers, mountains, water holes and distances. Every traveler should, in our opinion, have those maps.

The drive up the Vallee du Dra was every bit as spectacular as the drive down. You were just given a different perspective of the mud-brick, multi storied villages. How great it would have been to visit with those people, to live with them and get to really understand their views. They are Arabs, Moslems, and deeply religious people. It would be very difficult for us, with our training and indoctrination, to see and interpret the planet from their point of view.

From Ouarzazate the road took us east through Skoura. As we approached Skoura there were Ksars along both sides of the track. Between Skoura and El-Kelaa-des-Mgouna the Ksars were scattered until we reached Boumaine. That area supported a goodly number of people.

Every square foot of arable land seems to be intensely cultivated. Water, as well as land is being used to the limit—We often ask each other, with the population growing at about 3.8 %, what do they do with the "excess" people? The farms and gardens are very picturesque along the valley floors and terraced to the limit on the mountain sides—But, the people can not eat "picturesque!

## *GORGES DU DADES*

At Boumaine we turned north up the Gorges du Dades. There were several view points along the valley of jumbled, broken boulders. Vegetation was very sparse indeed! There were no garden plots to be seen. In fact, we did not see any other vehicles—And that made us a little cautious. There was no danger—Help was well within walking distance. (But, I did not want Emma to have to walk too far!!)

At a small village with the sign Msemrir we decided to head back to the main road to the east. The next "big town" would be Tinerhir. Tinerhir was a scenic center. There were several very attractive Ksars in Tinerhir and along the entrance to the Gorges du Todra.

Perhaps the best way to attempt to describe the Gorges would be to say that several scenes in "Laurence of Arabia "were shot there. The mountain is split forming sheer vertical walls so high and narrow that very little light makes it to the base of the valley each day, and then for a very short period of time!

Some water was flowing through the Gorge. It was quite shallow so-we were able to drive back and forth through the stream. The walls are hundreds of feet high! The color of the walls changes with the position of the sun—We spent the entire day just taking in the ever-changing panorama.

Unfortunately that could not be said of an English couple who also showed up in the Gorge! They had some trouble and their wind screen, as they called it, was broken—Not broken, it was gone! A piece of plastic did not help the situation. They were worried about that—But, they were much more worried about the "Arabs!" They could not explain why they were worried—The Arabs had done nothing to them. When they heard the story of our travels it was obvious that they did not believe us. Well, what could we do? Emma did her best to calm down the woman and I tried to talk to the man. Our efforts, I fear, fell upon deaf ears. They were headed for the nearest hotel—And England! Fortunately, they say, there will always be an England!

There was a pleasant spot along the water at the base of the Gorge. Looking back it was not a safe place to make camp! We knew that it is foolish to camp in any old, ravine, or dry river bed. But, the beauty of the place, the location got the better of our judgment. Obviously, there was no flash-flood that night—No heavy rain upstream. As I remember, we went to sleep listening to the water flow over the rough cracked and jagged valley floor. The large boulders that littered the stream bed should have sent me a message—They did not—That time we were just lucky!

The track toward the north end of the gorge became very rough—Rough even for that area! We had two spare tires on the front of the camper—That did not mean that we wanted to use them! We decided to turn back towards Tinerhir.

Near Tinerhir we followed what was marked on the map "scenic". Well, it was scenic—Uninhabited open desert—No ksars or palm trees. Within a few miles of travel eastward we were back on the main road to Goulmima and Ksar-es-Souk.

Goulmima was a crossroads and a center with various stores and open-air shops where Emma was able to do some shopping for fresh vegetables. When you have a one—burner stove, it seems, you eat a lot of vegetable stew. Sometimes Emma was able to find fresh meat. When available large chunks were hung on hooks in front of the shop. Emma said that the flies always found the meat before she did. I noticed that, when fresh meat was included with the vegetables, they were very well cooked!

The road east to Ksar-es-Souk was fairly good—Compared to some of the roads we had just been over. We remember seeing one mud-brick dwelling and a couple wells where water was available—That is, if you had your own bucket and a long rope. We had learned to keep both on hand for just such occasions.

At Ksar-es-Souk we turned north once again in order to pass through the Gorges du Ziz. The gorge did not have the spectacular vertical walls that Todra had—However, the valley of rough red stone was well worth the trip to see it. The stone changes color with the angle and intensity of the sunlight.

The track runs through the gorge north to the Legionnaires Tunnel. Of course that reminds one that Morocco was occupied by the French from about 1912 to 1956. Of greater interest to us were the little stone towers along the top of the top edge of the gorge. From those towers the French could keep a sharp eye on the activities of the restless valley residents.

On the way back to Ksar-es-Souk we talked about those towers and their significance. Their significance to the people who lived, and worked, in that valley! Because our country has never been occupied by a foreign power,(not since 1776) we could not have any concept of what it would be like! Emma commented, "Well, not to date but we should be careful!)

We were pleased to get back to Ksar-es—Souk. The road through the gorge was very rough—There was a bridge under construction. Our compensation for the rough road was more than paid for by the red rocky gorge and several view points. (From Ksar-es-Souk the track took us south to Source bleue de-Meski. There the clear water gushes out of a seam in the stone. It forms a large pool of sky-blue water. The crystal-clear water reflects the ever-present blue sky. Emma said, and I agreed, "This would be a great place to camp, and rest, for a few days." That was not to be."

Now, this is my side of the story,—the Arab is not here to offer his point of view. We were there a very short time. The Arab appeared and demanded money. We had no idea as to how much he was asking. There were no posted signs. His manner and dress did not give us the impression that he was "official. We tried to communicate with the few French and German words that we were mispronouncing—All to no avail! Finally, he looked at me and said "Departe." That French word, I told him in English, I did understand. And that is what we did!

The result was that we made camp at the first view point south of Source bleue de Meski. We had a great view down into, and over, the Ziz Valley. Early the following morning we continued on south toward Erfoud, Rissani, and the ancient Roman ruins of Sijilmassa

## *ZIZ VALLEY*

The track down through the Ziz Valley followed the Oued Ziz. The oasis extended all along the river. The Hammada du Guir spread out to the horizon on our left as we drove along. (I should say "bumped".) It was desolation at its best! Life followed the valley closely in the form of a thin ribbon. Emma described it best, I think—" It makes me think of an artery—The life-blood of all the different forms of life".

The ksars, mud buildings, were constructed on hill-tops, land that could not be cultivated. Many of the fields seemed to be irrigated—It looked like efficient, intensive farming. No land was wasted—The dense population would not permit it!

Beyond Erfoud the track took us into Rissani. The ksars were not as numerous as they had been north of Erfoud. Anyway, we were mainly interested in getting to Rissani, the last stop before entering the Sahara!—That is providing you have all the required knowledge and equipment.

To us, the ancient Roman ruins were not quite as spectacular as we had imagined. That was not because of the information provided—But, because we were thinking of Rome and Tunisia. The history of the area, we thought, was more interesting than the actual ruins.

The ruins are in an area called Sijilmassa, a Roman outpost all caravans, all trade, anything that moved through the area, was controlled. It was a toll station—Maybe one of the first! The city became very wealthy.

If I got the story right—By about 1500 the nomads of the desert got organized—They sacked the city! The only thing left were the ruins as we saw them.

Rissani is the ancestral home of the present dynasty that has reigned for the past three hundred years. I believe the present king maintains a residence in the area. It does not seem easy for a tourist passing through to acquire accurate information relating to the various dynasties. From what we were able to gather Morocco has had a very checkered history when it comes to who was in charge, when, and for how long! We were told that the present government has some very serious enemies. We did learn, years past that it is very unwise for foreigners to get involved in local affairs.

From Rissani it is possible to travel farther into the desert. We were told that a rough track leads to a village called Merzouga. In that area one can experience genuine Saharan scenery. Since we were on our way into the Sahara Proper we decided not to attempt it. The decision was made to turn around and head north through Erfoud and Source bleue de Meski. We did that—But, as you might guess, we did not stop over at Source bleue de Meski!! At Source bleue we made the right turn and headed east toward Boudenib. The track was fairly good. Although Emma had shopped at several open markets there were some things that we thought we should pick up before we crossed the border into Algeria.

The latest news indicated that there was considerable unrest in Algeria. That meant that we might not be allowed into the country after all. "Well", Emma said "We have had a great trip across Morocco, we can return by another route, maybe head north, it could be just as interesting". It was not at all difficult for me to agree with her. In fact, I would not have objected to following the same tracts back!

## *BOUDENIB AND AN ADVENTURE WITH THREE FRENCHMEN*

The tract to Boudenib had one well, according to the Michelin Map, located about half way across. There were a few mud houses not far from the well—And the usual ample supply of children of all ages. They were well-behaved. They tried to help us get water from the well. Emma engineered the entire enterprise. She was not very adept at using the goat—skinned water bucket! Several of the older children jumped at the chance to assist. They all laughed and enjoyed the whole adventure. There were so many of them! What would they do when they grew up! There were already far too many mouths for the limited resources available!

Not far from the well we found a wide place along the road and decided to stop for the night. We were not far from the village but we were alone—Nothing in sight. There was no traffic. The table was lowered, Emma took up her central position between the table and the 'range", our one-burner cook-stove. In a short time the stew was cooking—Again! It was a great space-saving arrangement—Neither of us had to move during the entire operation!

When we finished eating and the two bowls and spoons had been washed we decided to check the Michelin maps. That was done frequently as I have mentioned. A few miles east of Boudenib a track leading north was indicated. It was green indicating that it would be scenic. There were also dark dots along the road. We did not take note of them.

The decision was made to drive up that way and check out the scenery. The usual procedure was followed. The maps were rolled up, put up on a shelf over the back seat, the table hooked to the wall, the bed pulled out, sleeping bags rolled out—And two tired, sleepy travelers were asleep. To our knowledge, nothing outside, or inside for that matter, moved during the night.

In the morning, after our usual bowel of oatmeal, the very dusty camper was again bouncing along the track toward Boudenib. A few miles east of Boudenib we came upon the track leading north.

Within a few miles we learned, the hard way, what those dark dots along the road meant. The area was indeed very scenic! It was also very rough, and just plain dangerous! Steep drop-offs and no guard rails were all along the track. There were fairly large, jagged, rocks around which we tried to make our way. The decision to turn around presented no problem! The problem was to find a place in which the maneuver might be carried out without going over the bank.

Emma got out in order to give directions. She said it was necessary so that I did not back onto a soft spot. I did not mention the fact that she was also safer on the ground and out of the vehicle! Once again we were on our way into Boudenib.

Emma had to shop. She shopped frequently in order to get fresh food. We carried enough canned and dried food to last a week or more, and plenty of water and extra fuel. But, there was no refrigeration! It was necessary to adapt and eat whatever was available. If, like one man we talked to in an up-scale hotel, you required stewed prunes every morning, then this was not the type trip that you should undertake!

By the time we arrived in the small village all the shops were open. Some consisted of sheep, chickens, goats, etc., displayed on the ground in the central square. Other shops were in buildings with open-air fronts. The people were interesting, and very friendly. We were identified as foreigners by language and dress instantly. It seems to be a "law" that everyone does everything possible to make guests feel at ease. We did!

While Emma was shopping, and I was looking everything, and everyone over, she found two French girls who spoke perfect English. I say "perfect" because their pronunciation and grammar was much better than mine.

They said that they, and their husbands, were there working as teachers. We did not ask questions relating to financial arrangements. And that also applies to marital status!

Just as we were about to leave their husbands arrived. They were curious about us and our journey—And our intended venture into the Sahara.

Southern Morocco seemed to be enough desert for them. Probably it would satisfy most normal people!

It must have been two or three PM by the time we were ready to depart. Someone suggested that we all have super together! It sounded like a great idea to us. Emma would give the one-burner a rest—And we might get a taste of local food. The decision was made to meet in front of a local "restaurant" about 6PM.

All the roads, tracks, and streets were sand—And dust! We located one that seemed to circle the village and followed it. A mile or so from the village there was an airfield. It did not appear to be very modern—But, we only saw it from the road. Across from the airfield the track turned south, then west—At least according to our compass. It was a desert track and that is for sure!

Our maps indicated that the Sahara did not really begin until the Algerian border was crossed. Well, it appeared to us that we were in the desert as we drove along the track from Source bleue de Meski. We were on the northern edge of the Hammada du Guir, an empty land devoid of visible plant or animal life. However, we were to learn later that, in the desert, appearances can be, and are, very deceiving!

Along the rough track we did see two attractive Ksour or mud homes of extended families. They appear to be quite complicated from the outside. As the family expands additions are made All of mud brick and grass matting. There are very few windows, and those that are installed are small, usually decorated around the outside. The decorations have some religious or spiritual significance. Most of the life activities and work is carried out on the flat rooftops. We saw the women working and the children playing—I do not remember seeing anything that might prevent a child, dog, goat, or chicken from falling two or three stories!

At one point, near the end of the loop there were some ruins. We were late for our supper date and I certainly did not want to miss that! We thought that we would be able to return to the ruins—But, that was not to be.

Upon our arrival our new friends were waiting. They had moved two tables out of the restaurant into the street. That did not seem to create any problem for the occasional man with a donkey or a camel. They passed without a second glance, seemed to take no notice of the four of us eating in the middle of the street!

We had what I would call stew!! Yes, stew! But, this time it was different. It was full of fresh vegetables and meat, lots of meat. Emma tried to find out exactly what might be in the stew—If she got a direct answer I missed it. My guess is that it was camel meat. Why they might not have wanted to tell us we do not know. Of course they had no way of knowing that, on our motorcycle tour through Europe and North Africa, we ate plenty of horse meat.

The stew was delicious—And I mean that! The unleavened flat bread, baked in an oven behind the restaurant was also still hot and tasty. Everything was topped off with a variety of very sweet cakes and hot, very hot, sweet tea. I thought of staying right there! Emma said, "If you ate like that every day you might not be able to get into and out of the camper!"

I was so busy eating and enjoying the food that I did not notice one of the young men had disappeared. He soon returned driving what might be described as a home-made desert buggy. In order to get any accurate concept of the vehicle you have to refer to the picture of me behind the wheel.

Everyone climbed in, or hung on as best he could, and we headed out into the desert—The Hammada Du Guir. In the desert night with the stars brighter than we have ever seen them, we sped over the dunes and across the seemingly endless Hammada. From some bushes unidentified birds took flight. Pairs of shining eyes flashed in the glare of the headlights. An owl passed overhead indicating that there were enough mice present to keep him alive and curious as to what the disturbance might be about. One of the men investigated several of the bushes—Curled up under one he pointed out a fat rattle snake! We all decided not to disturb him any farther!

We all knew that there were enough insects in and around the bushes for the birds and mice. One lizard was out hunting—And being hunted! There was far more life in the so-called "lifeless" desert than there appears to be.

Everyone clambered back aboard and we were off into the desert blackness. I thought we were headed back toward the village. We were headed farther out into the hammada. Without proper compass bearings you are lost in the desert—Unless you are a Nomad or a Taureg.

Our driver knew exactly where he was. After some distance, slowly, a large Ksar emerged out of the blackness. There were no outside lights. You had to know where the narrow entrance was located. Our hosts had small flashlights, and along the narrow dark passage there were two or three torches burning.

Finally, we entered a rather large room. It was located deep inside the Ksar, The floor was carpeted and so were the walls. We all removed our shoes. From the side, from behind one of the beautiful hanging carpets several women appeared. Each one wore a hat, really a head-dress, and floor-length robes. The robes were not "Arab", they were designs of the local tribe—I suspect the design of the local Berber Tribe or clan. We could not get that information.

As the women sang they were accompanied by several men playing stringed instruments and others playing flutes. Some of the flutes appeared to be hand-carved.

At the end of the dancing and the music the area suddenly cleared. A thick carpet was unrolled and we were invited to sit down. An elderly man wearing a heavy burnoose with the hood pulled up appeared and joined us. The teachers were able to talk with him in the local dialect.

As they talked, two young girls appeared with trays of cookies and the usual small glasses of sweet tea. Everyone obviously enjoyed the evening.

The elderly gentleman escorted us back through the entrance passage. While shaking hands you are to allow your fingers to slide over the other persons palm and then touch your heart. You do not try to crush his fingers!

We thought that the performance was unique. We were special guests! We were very moved by the entire spectacle. The culture and the music were foreign to us—With no background how could we really appreciate it? We did our best to thank everyone.

Two ignorant Americans—Not enough background to really appreciate what we had seen and heard—And, we could not even say "Thank you" in their language! How could the average American ever be capable of understanding and being able to appreciate the culture of such people?

The desert buggy was cranked up and we all piled in—We were off into the night and absolute blackness. Again the headlights picked up some of the desert denizens.

It was quite late, the temperature in the desert drops very quickly as soon as the sun sets. The citizens of the desert wear the heavy burnoose as protection from the sun during the day and the bitter cold during the night.

Suddenly the driver stopped near a large bush. Everybody jumped out. Emma and I had no idea as to what might happen next. We soon found out! With a lighted match, one man touched a branch of the bush. It burst into flame! The headlights had been switched off—We all stood around the burning bush. The light was bright, probably because of the stark contrast with the desert blackness. An astronomer would have really been able to appreciate the display that the stars put on!

The bush burnt out, the heat disappeared, and the desert cold cut through, seemingly, to your very bones! Back into the buggy and to Boudenib!

We all shook hands, said our good-by's, and parted. Emma and I had enjoyed a real desert adventure! All we could say was thank you—And good-bye. We appreciated what everyone had done, but we were sad. Sad that it was over and disappointed that we were incapable of showing our appreciation. People like that make, even a skeptic, wonder??

Back in the camper, along the side of the track, we sat and discussed what had happened for a long time. We usually get to bed at an early hour.

The track out of Boudenib was not very good—It was rough! But, for a few miles, it was scenic. There were a couple forts or bordj and cultivated gardens. After that it was just plain rough!

There was no traffic headed for Figuig, the border crossing. Figuig is an oasis but it is off the main line. There were several wells along the way, but, we did not need any water.

At a village named Bouanane a track ran to a fort near a village called Takoumit. The track on the map looked rough but, we thought it would be out of the way, and interesting.

At Bouanane we made the turn north! Bad idea! The track was a little more than rough—It was impossible—Even for a VW! We did have two extra tires—But only two! We wanted to have two extra tires—Not two, or more, broken tires. The decision to turn around was very easy.

The track remained very rough all the way to the village of Mangoub where there was another fort or bordj. Mangoub was nothing more than a cross-roads. Nothing there except the fort.

# FIGUIG

The decision was made to take the short-cut, it seemed to be only a few miles—And, we would be at the oasis of Figuig earlier. The map is indispensable—But, it can not really indicate the conditions on the track. We did have previous experiences with short-cuts!

As mentioned, the map clearly indicated that we were traveling along the north edge of the Hammada Du Guir. Hammadas are made up of broken, polished, sun-baked stone and sand. The short-cut lived up to that description—And then some!

A few miles down the track a branch went to the south. Just a short distance away we could see a bordj. It appeared to be built on rocky ledge surrounded by absolutely nothing! There was no sign of any kind of life. It was in good repair so it must have been occupied. Nomads live in the area and they are not in residence the year round. Their location is determined by the seasons, the rains, and the condition of pastures in the area.

Back on the main track we continued toward Figuig. Within a few more rocky miles the main track appeared. Compared to what we had just crossed I think that I should refer to it as a road!

As we approached the oasis the desert did not seem so hostile. We thought that it might seem that way because we knew that the village, and people, were nearby. There was an excellent view point on the left and a bordj. Every view point had to be kept in mind just in case parking in the village became a problem.

Figuig was a much larger oasis than we had expected. There is a large expanse of water. Well, after the desert, it might have seemed larger. There are many tall palm trees and low-growing vegetation. Ducks were on the pond and many birds flying about. Flocks of birds migrate across the desert. However, if I were one of their number, I very well might stay. It is many, many miles across the Sahara and the mortality rate is very high.

The hotel looked inviting. It was set in a palm grove. Built of mud brick, it seemed to blend into the landscape. There was ample parking space in the back—That meant that, if all went well, we would not have to drive back out to the view-point we passed on the way in.

There were several Land Rovers, and also a few Japanese four wheel drive vehicles parked in the lot. While there are still many Vws in the desert—They are being replaced by Japanese models. I never got to drive the VW Synchro, a four wheel drive van, it seemed to be a great idea!

It was getting late. We decided to try parking behind the hotel. We planned to have breakfast at the hotel in the morning.

The night passed without incident—At least as far as we were concerned. We walked around to the front entrance of the hotel. There were stately palm trees, low shrubbery, and flowering plants. The possibilities were endless—Plenty of water was available. The area was quite a contrast to the hammada that we had been living in!

As I remember it, the inside was quite plain. It was well lighted, but offered no view. There were attractive carpets on the walls and floors. The dining area was small, but probably more than adequate for the number of diners.

When we decided upon a table the waiter appeared wearing a white apron and a red fez. (Arab style hat.) We ordered a bowl of cereal of some type. I have no idea what it might have been. I ordered coffee. (The sweet, hot tea was very enjoyable—But, we were ready for a cup of coffee.)

While we were waiting for our order to arrive two men appeared. They had been sitting at a bar in the back of the room. They were well dressed—Obviously for the desert. Their leather boots must have cost plenty. Safari-type pants, shirts, and wide-brimmed hats completed their outfits.

They spoke English, French, and Arabic! The conversation first turned to our journey, and our plans. They had seen us arrive and park behind the hotel. (And we thought no one had known about our presence!)

They were French geologists working for a corporation prospecting for oil in the Sahara. At the moment they were on leave or vacation. Because of the conditions in the desert the schedule seems to be that you work for a couple weeks, then you have the same amount of vacation time. Usually they fly directly from the oil field to Paris. This time they had to lay over in Figuig for a few days. There was a problem with the plane.

It seemed that they wanted to talk to us. We thought later that, having spent several weeks in the desert, they enjoyed visiting with a couple strange Americans.

We learned that they are provided with Hugh, self-contained trailers in which they live at the work site. Everything is provided, cook, laundry, garbage disposal, you name it! The mobile homes are moved around in the desert by huge diesel-powered tractors. There are also library facilities and movies. Also mentioned was an off-duty open bar! I wanted to inquire about "girls" but did not have the nerve. (I am still curious!)

Emma brought up the key question—"Who pays for all this? Is it not very expensive? Their answer was something of a surprise!

They both answered, "You do! America pays everything!" They went on to explain—" We are French, we occupied Algeria—But we managed to get out gracefully, without too much ill feeling. You Americans, on the other hand have managed to antagonize the present government. You are not allowed to prospect for oil in Algeria." The bottom line was that the French do the prospecting and the Americans pay the bill!

After that bomb was dropped the conversation turned to our plans in the Sahara. They did not try to discourage us. They did advise extreme caution. Specifically they advised us not to travel into the Western Sahara because of the Polisaro Gorillas. The Polisaro, Algeria, and Morocco are squabbling over the Western Sahara—It is the oil and gas that they are all after-Greed.!

The Polisaro likes to take hostages. They can make money and gain national attention that way. We had no plans to travel in the Western Sahara!

We were told to report our presence to the "Perfect" in every town and village of any size. The Perfect functions something like the mayor and chief of police, all in one person. We were to learn that he is, indeed, the head man in the town!

It is not permitted to travel in the Southern desert without the permission of the Perfect in the town where you enter. For us that would be Figuig.

The prospectors told us that several people in a touring car had entered the desert by way of Figuig undetected. They had no water, and no food. The vehicle broke down, no spare parts—They died of thirst after trying to drink oil from the motor!

On that happy note we parted from the prospectors. They gave us additional information relating to the geology of the Sahara. It probably would be best to use that when we are in the desert.

The conversation had run late into the day. Another day of crystal blue skies! Back in the camper again we made a tour of the oasis. The large pond, or lake, reflected the palm trees, the vegetation, and the blue sky. The scene made us think about heading out into the sand dunes and rocky hammada. But, Ain Salah was our goal and we were determined to get there—Or else!

We returned to our parking spot behind the hotel. Emma made stew—What else!? We went to bed—In the morning we would drive over to the Algerian Border Post! The question that had followed us all the way from Rabat would finally be answered—Would we be able to enter the Sahara?

Our stay of just a few days in Figuig had been very pleasant, we were hesitant about leaving. When you are traveling in foreign lands and facing unknown potential problems it is probably natural to experience feelings of insecurity. That feeling may keep the majority of people from venturing too far from home. Although we did experience such feelings we were able to overcome them and move on.

*Camper being loaded on the freighter in Casablanca*

*Rearranging everything after getting off the freighter*

*Camped 4 days on the street in Rabat while waiting for our visa to Algeria*

*SQUARE JENNAA EL FNA IN MARRAKESH, A circus of entertainment*

*Dancers from Mauritania would swing tassels around their head as they danced*

*A bus pulled this mobile home for German travelers.*

*A close up of a Ksar showing roof top apartments*

*Our map indicated that this well had good drinking water.*
*The boys came from out of no where to help*

*Two children were tied on the back of two camels
while their parents collected herbs and food.*

*Valley Du Dra on the edge of the Great Sahara.*

*In the desert night, with the stars brighter than we have ever seen them,*
*we crossed the seemingly endless Hammada.*

*A road scene in the Atlas Mountains.*

*A Taureg parked his white camel in the center of the square as he shopped*

*We helped dig the Germans out of the soft sand, while traveling in convoy.*

*A stop for fuel and water*

*A man was carrying his lamb because the sand was to hot
for the animal to walk*

*The sand was slowly moving over the village of Beni Abbes.*

*Unique Fulcrum well in Beni Abbes.*

*Checking our route through the most dangerous section
of the Sahara with the Germans*

*A building used to sell slaves who had been marched across the desert in chains.
Only a few survived the trip.*

*Ain Salah where travelers from around the world*
*stopped to make repairs and rest*

*The one bar in Ain Salah. The only safe drink was a bottle of beer.*

*Road into Ain Salah blocked by a sand dune*

*The beetle collects dew on his body. As it condenses he drinks it.*

*Figuig the border to Algeria*

# FIGUIG TO AIN SALAH

When Emma and I traveled through Morocco and Algeria we were free to roam about the countries and the villages. When dusk fell we pulled to the side of the track and made camp as has been described. In Algeria, in 1969-70 we were still able to travel in that manner.

In Algeria now freedom of travel, as we did it, is not permitted. It is very difficult to secure a visa. If, after a satisfactory explanation, one is issued, you are no longer permitted to travel freely and alone. A certified, licensed guide must accompany you at all times. The guide instructs you as to what you can and can not photograph, where you are permitted to travel, etc. The guide must be in your vehicle at all times.

Emma and I have traveled throughout Europe, Scandinavia, Turkey, North, South, East, and Central Africa. We traveled by VW Camper and we were free to go where we wished. The only time we had any difficulty with the authorities was in Communist Bulgaria, Yugoslavia, and East Berlin.

It is relatively easy to have difficulty using a camera in any country where the authorities have something to hide. In the communist countries it was repression of the citizens. When the local natives are restless, deprived, crowded, hungry, and feel restricted, the authorities have very good reason to feel threatened.

When those in control feel insecure, the repressive measures are increased. Although Emma and I have never had any "secret" motives or agenda, it would be impossible for us to even attempt to travel with a guide in the vehicle!

The Algerian border post was austere. As we approached it we both had feelings of uneasiness, a strange feeling of really being on our own in a very vast and lonely country. Perhaps those feelings were the result of the reading and research that we had done on the Sahara. They were not due to anything that we had experienced in Algeria because we had not yet entered the country. Emma said, "See how easy it is to form an opinion on the basis of no facts?"

In the desert things are not always what they appear to be. That lesson was made clear later when we camped for the night. It is possible to travel great distances and not see another living person. After that, at dusk, we would pull off the track and camp. In the morning you might pull back the curtains and see several Arabs just standing around looking at the camper, and probably listening to us talk and make breakfast inside. They probably came from a village several miles off the track. Many of the villages were so well camouflaged that we did not see them unless they were very close to the track. The buildings are low, one-story, built of mud bricks that blend into the surrounding desert sands.

The border-post building stood alone in an open, sandy area. It really did appear lonely and austere. The mud walls and rusty tin roof gave the impression of a lack of interest, finances, or governmental concern. There was no gate or barrier of any kind and no one was outside. I had the distinct feeling that it made no difference whether we stopped or went on our way. We stopped and went in by way of an old, weathered, and warped door.

Two men in uniform were in the large, barren room. One sat in a wooden straight-backed chair, the other behind a plain small wood table. There were no papers on the table and, no files visible. Neither man stood up, smiled, or offered to shake hands, or be friendly in any way. No one said anything. I thought it best to present our pass-ports. The man behind the desk appeared to me to take a very cursory glance at our papers and followed that with gesture that indicated we should proceed.

Once outside we looked at each other. Emma smiled and said, "Well, Ted, here we are in the Sahara Desert at last!"

From our trusty Michelin Maps we knew that we should head south toward a village called Bechar. That village is known as "The entrance to the Sahara." Since there was an unlimited amount of open space we decided to pull to the side of the sandy track and camp for the night. It certainly appeared to be safe enough, there was only sand and stony ground to be seen. It was early in the day but we had to check the maps, especially the track south of Bechar. Emma had dried food and as much canned food as we could safely carry. The gasoline, oil, and water tanks were full. We were as ready to head out on the track to Ain Salah as we would ever be!

The Sahara Desert is very large expanse of sand, stone, and, in the south massive mountains. Many people have the mistaken impression that it is an area of pure sand. Actually the Sahara consists of only one sixth sand. The sand seas are called ergs. The rest of the desert is mostly what the Arabs call reg. The reg consists of thousands of square miles of small stones that have been washed out onto the desert floor by flash-floods originating in the mountains. It is good to keep in mind that when the Sahara is referred to one is talking about an area roughly the size of the United States! It is the second largest desert in the world. Just as important, it has the reputation of being the most inhospitable environment for life on the planet earth. Anyone contemplating a trip of any kind into the Sahara should have those facts firmly in mind, they should prepare with great care and caution. Too frequently they do not.

In spite of the warning signs, the border posts, and the system of checking travelers at every village, some people ignore everything and drive out into the desert! Just as we arrived four French visitors drove past the check stations and out into the desert. They had made absolutely no preparations!

In the desert the temperatures often drops to below freezing, 22 F. During the heat of day the cloudless blue sky shows no mercy, the temperature can rise to 136 F!! Exposed to that heat no form of life is able to survive without a plentiful supply of water or some means of dealing with the heat. Some animals have altered, adapted their metabolism, some hide, or burrow into the sand. A few desert tribes have, over many generations, adapted to life in the desert. It is a surprise to some people to learn that many forms of life have adapted to those harsh conditions.

The camel immediately comes to mind. The camel has had many hundreds of years during which it has slowly been able to adapt to desert conditions. It has a thick protective coat that prevents the accumulation of excessive heat. Its metabolism is able to adjust as required to external factors. Limited amounts of vital water can be stored and food in the form of fat is provided in the famous hump. The camel has additional adaptive features—that is the practical value of such long legs? All they do is make it difficult for us to mount and dismount! Not at all! Those long legs have definite survival value under desert conditions. The bulk of the body is raised up high above the surface of the sand or reg. The most intense heat is at the surface. The almost constant hot wind blows over the surface, about the first two feet above ground level. That hot air is laden with fine sand, sand that blasts and polishes everything in its path. If you stand out in the open you soon become aware of this. If you sit down and try to eat you will eat some sand. It is much better to stand up!

The camel is only one of many forms of life that have adapted to desert conditions. On our safari from Figuig to Ain Salah we were to observe many examples of evolutionary adaptations, plant and animal, including desert nomads of the human variety.

To return to the story of the foolish four French tourists—The incident had just occurred along the track that we planned to take to Ain Salah. It is plainly indicated on the Michelin map as dangerous, with no available water. Even if water is indicated on your map you must note how deep the well is and, of course, have a rope long enough to reach it. (And a container.) (And purification equipment.)

We could not learn what stopped them—Out of fuel? Motor trouble and no spare parts? No radiator water? They became stalled between Adrar, one of the hottest places in the Sahara, and their destination, probably Ain Salah. The blazing sun of the Sahara shows no mercy. It was not known how many days they were stranded. It was learned that they attempted to drink water from the cooling system. Unfortunately, none of them survived the ordeal.

The Sahara is not unique in demanding extensive planning and preparation. When we traveled north through Norway beyond the Arctic

Circle and into Lapland the preparations were quite different but, just as important. The same must be said about travel through Central Africa and the Congo.

An adventure might be described as an event that takes place when you least expect it or when you have not made the proper preparations. Some adventures can not be avoided but, many could have been. When something unexpected happens, the best thing to do is stay calm so that you are able to think and react.

The area around Figuig was heavily fortified. As far as we could see in either direction barbed wire was strung upon upright triangles of steel posts driven into the sand. Along the top was coiled razor wire! On either side of the fence were land-mines. Morocco and Algeria were, and had been, at odds over the Western Sahara.
Neither country wanted the land area as such, what they wanted was the potential oil reserves and the mineral deposits.

As tourists we were not concerned about such local matters. We were concerned when we learned that certain desert tribesmen had taken hostages. Their goal was to collect ransom money. Some people thought that the Polisaro was directing their operations. We simply did not want to get involved. One man said the best way to not get involved would be to stay away from the Western Sahara.

In Morocco there were many different tribes, each with its own distinctive way of life. The one thing they all had in common was the Moslem Faith. Even as devout Moslems they each clung to their own interpretation of that faith. Emma said, "They are just like the Christians." I agreed. About the only thing that the Christians agree upon is that they are Christians. How many different sects, groups, or what have you, among the Christians all claim to worship the same God? The same God that the Moslems claim to worship.

If all the different Arab groups could unite under one banner, the Arabs would form a force in the world that would be invincible. From what we have been able to observe in North Africa, that potential world force lies in the very distant future.

The track from Figuig toward Bechar was in fine shape. We were able to make good time. (That is, for us) We passed one impressive ksar or fortified red-mud village along a dra or dry river bed. Just a few miles beyond it was an impressive view-point that overlooks the Hammada du Guir, the sand and rock-strewn wasteland that runs between Morocco and Algeria. The track runs along the dry river bed and the famous railroad that the French started to build across Africa. The railroad was intended to run from the Mediterranean Coast in Algeria to the coast in West Africa. It was a very ambitious project! It could have been done and it would have united the French Empire in West Africa. The first railroad across the Sahara! It was not to be. The colonies in North Africa demanded their freedom. The grand railroad that would have crosses the Sahara and united the French Empire in West Africa made it to just a few miles beyond Bechar! In a sandy, isolated area the tracks ended just short of a village named Abadia. There, in the sandy wastes of the Sahara, the two rusty iron rails protrude from the slowly forming sand dune. The grand dream is dead, soon it will be buried, like all the dreams of man, by the eternal sands of the Sahara.

Bechar is the administrative center of a western province. The palm trees along the dry wadi (erratic water course) present a welcome sight. We drove through the traditional and European areas. That is as close as we could to the traditional areas. There were many shops and stores. Bechar is the staging area for some trips into the Sahara. The name of the village is taken from a 1600 foot mountain nearby. We passed the train station and what appeared to be a newspaper office. When Emma saw the newspaper office she remarked "Didn't Isabella work here for some time as a journalist?"

Isabella did work in Bechar as a journalist! She was a woman socially far ahead of the times in which she lived. Her mother was married to a Russian General. Apparently the marriage gave each partner considerable freedom. Isabella's mother left Russia for Switzerland, taking a tutor with her. The tutor happened to be an anarchist ex-priest, Alexander Trophinosky.

Isabella was born in Switzerland and registered as illegitimate. At about the same time (1877) the General in Russia died because of a heart attack. Isabella grew up in Switzerland and was tutored by Trophinosky. He must have been an excellent tutor. Isabella learned metaphysics, chemistry, and several languages. She was fluent in Arabic, could read and write it professionally. She had a masterly grasp of Arab culture and history.

There was another side to Isabella. She became a cross-dressing, hard-drinking, fast-living individual. In 1897 Isabella made her first trip to Algeria. She liked Algeria very much, felt at home there. Although she returned to Switzerland briefly, she soon returned to Algeria.

She assumed the person of an Arab man. She felt that a man's clothing gave her more freedom. In Algeria it very likely did just that. Isabella was well-known throughout the Sahara and, it was widely known and accepted, that she was really a woman. She
Traveled alone and on horseback.

About 1900 she fell in love and married. Fortunately he was the type man who could accept her wild life-style, her absence, and her bouts of drinking.

In 1904 she was being treated for malaria in a village on the edge of the Sahara known as Ain Sefra. Released from the hospital, Isabella returned to the free life out in the desert. To understand her fascination with the desert one must have lived there for some time.

She met her fate during a freak flash-flood. Her body was found some days later wedged under a log. Isabella is buried in the cemetery in Ain Sefra.

Upon arrival in Bechar the correct procedure is to report to the prefect. He is the local authority and, in Algeria he wants to know just about everything that is taking place in his village. Not reporting would arouse suspicion. We made our way into his office. It appeared neater, more organized by far than the border post.

The Prefect sat behind a well-organized desk. There were several types of official papers neatly filed along one side. He checked our papers, seemed satisfied, and rolled back away from the desk. When he got up and walked to the window to look at the camper we were able to get a better look at him. He was of medium height and build. He appeared rather thin but muscular, well coordinated, and in excellent physical condition. He had a military bearing. His English was very good.

He said, "If you are going to travel to Ain Salah you will have to do so in convoy of at least two well-equipped vehicles." We described our supplies of food, water, fuel, and spare-parts. He seemed pleased, but stressed, "You must have at least two vehicles and one of you must have sand-tracks."

Sand-tracks are perforated, steel metal plates about eight feet long. When the vehicle sinks into soft sand it must be cleared between the front and rear wheels. The sand-tracks are laid down and the idea is to get the rear wheels up on the tracks. Obviously it does not always work the first time. We were to learn that from several personal experiences! (The tracks can also be made from heavy wire, even chicken wire will help—but not much!) We needed to find another vehicle, properly equipped, on its way to Ain Salah!

The hotel was one possibility, the coffee shops presented others. The first two days passed without any results. Our spirits began to fade. We ask each other, "What are the odds of someone passing through Bechar on his way to Ain Salah in the Sahara? We knew that the Prefect would not allow us to proceed without another vehicle. Not only that, it had to be fairly well equipped! The evening of the second day we were talking about alternate routes. The idea of turning back at this stage of the journey did not set well.

The morning of the third day, at breakfast, we sat looking at each other. We really did not know what to do. We drove into the village and pulled up in front of a mud-walled Arab coffee shop. While we were parked there passing the time, a VW van drove in and parked alongside of us. The van had water and fuel containers on the roof. It had sand-tracks lashed to one side. The registration plates were German. Three young men jumped out and walked over to our camper.

They were Germans, we learned, on their way to West Africa! That was good news but, we knew that there were three main trans-Saharan routs. Which one did they plan to take? Everyone sat around an old wooden table just outside the coffee shop door.

They were students who decided to take some time off and head for an adventure in the Sahara. The Prefeect had told them that we were in the village and seeking another vehicle properly equipped, on its way toAin Salah. So, they were looking for us!

Our supplies had been checked and double-checked, we were ready to start. They had some last-minute shopping to do and, they needed to completely fill their water and fuel containers. Something that we thought should have been done farther north. We were in no position to question them, another vehicle was required. The decision was made to start out early the next morning.

The next village of any size would be Beni-Abbes. That one was located some distance off the track and, probably would not have anything that we might need. Our best objective would be Adrar, an administrative center. Adrar had an air field, a first-aid station, and a radio communications station.

The communications center was very important. The centers are located at strategic points along each trans-Saharan track. They are in constant radio contact with each other. That is why it is very important for trans-Saharan travelers to stop in every village of any size and report to the Prefect. We would be traveling south from Bechar. Bechar would radio the next village, Beni-Abbes, that we left. When we reach Beni-Abbes Bechar would be notified that we had arrived. If a vehicle fails to arrive within a reasonable period of time a search vehicle is dispatched.

The system operates very efficiently if all travelers cooperate. If travelers do not report as requested it causes considerable expense and frustration. It should be obvious that, if the authorities do not know you are out there, they can not send out search parties.

Our trans-Saharan safari left Bechar the following morning. We traveled south-east over a mixture of sand and small gravel-like areas. On our right a low weathered out-crop of sand-blasted crumbling rock extended toward the south and west. On our left, to the east we noticed the beginning dunes of the Grand Erg Occidental, a vast sea of beautiful sand dunes that covered many hundreds of square miles. Several days could have been spent exploring the accessible dune formations. Primitive tracks led off in various directions. Emma remarked that we were passing a great deal of spectacular scenery. We had the desire, and the time, to explore, but the Germans either did not, or, more likely had no interest. We all had to stay together! Well, as much together as was physically possible!

The young Germans exhibited no interest in the rocky out-crops or the vast, spectacular sea of sand. Fortunately we had our compass set on Adrar and we would arrive there with, or without, them! I doubt that they took the time to drive into Beni-Abbes and report to the Perfect—so we did. By that time they were gone down the sandy rock-strewn track, out of sight.

Beni-Abbes is an oasis village. It is located on the edge of a rocky outcrop and has a view of a local palmeriae and the oued. While we were looking for the office of the Perfect we did get a glimpse of several old, arched, faded buildings. The village is surrounded by very high dunes!

From our guide-books we knew that Beni-Abbes was the site selected by Charles de Foucald for his first hermitage The remains are still there but we did not have time to locate them. Foucald was a religious hermit who sought solitude, first in Beni-Abbes, then in a crude structure that he built in the Hoggar Mountains farther south in the desert.

Foucald (1858-1916) was born into a wealthy French family. He was very fond of the good life and enjoyed parties and drinking. When he tired of the high life he decided to join the army. However, he was always short on self-discipline and he soon deserted. Disguising himself as a rabbi, he set off to explore the hill country of Morocco. Impressed by the Moslem religion he returned to France and after several years was ordained as a priest. He then returned to North Africa, this time to Beni-Abbes, then Tamanrasset in the south of the Sahara, and finally to the Hoggar Mountains even farther south and more remote.

Christianity was not popular in the Sahara. During his lifetime he managed to convert one person. He built a primitive hermitage in the mountains and managed to survive there for years. He learned much about the Tuareg and their culture. He compiled a dictionary in the French-Tamashek languages.

Foucald kept in touch with the outside world by way of written letters carried by local tribesmen. When the mail was delivered he had the habit of extending his arm out of a small opening in order to receive it. During a rebellion in 1916, a group of rebels who had learned of his location and his habit of collecting his mail, approached the hermitage one night. Thinking that it was his mail being delivered, Foucald extended his arm. His arm was cut off with one swipe of the blade and he was killed. The rebels thought that Foucald was part of a French plot to infiltrate the Sahara. His body is buried in El-Golea.

When we arrived at the track leading to the east to Timimoun we had no idea as to which way they might have gone. We calculated that judging by their speed they would head straight for Adrar. Our guess was correct, we found them parked just beyond the turn-off. Everyone got out and we tried to discuss the events of the day.

Ideas could be exchanged—with patience. Our German was very, very basic. Two of the young men spoke no English at all. The third, Dieter, had a fair mastery of the language. The exchange of all information had to go through Dieter. The concept of slowing down did not seem to translate very well. So, we were very pleased that we had invested in the compass. In the future we were to be even more pleased!

The decision was made to camp where we were and head on into Adrar the following morning. There was no traffic, nothing moved that night on the track. But, in the early morning there was evidence of activity during the night. During the night there was the sound of an owl hooting. If an owl was in the area he had to have food-probably in the form of small rodents. Some tufts of grass could be found and, around the base of them the tracks of what I thought to be mice. That, and the tracks of birds indicated the presence of insects. Looking for bugs was out of the question-the German Panzer Division was ready to move upon Adrar!

South of Beni-Abbes our convoy ran into its first encounter with desert problems! The track passed through part of the Grand Erg Occidental. It was a dune area of sand that covered the track. Emma and I had encountered sandy areas in southern Morocco. We were advised to keep a sharp eye out for any color changes as we approached. Soft sand has a slightly darker surface but you must be looking for it.

As we approached the Panzer VW it was obvious as to what had happened. They tried to accelerate as they got closed to the sand and force their way through. If they had a powerful land rover with sand tires partly deflated it could have been done with ease. But, not with a VW sporting a 40 Hp. Engine!

A brief inspection of the area quickly revealed more firm sand off to the west-And also the fact that another vehicle had recently discovered it. The sand tracks had to be unlashed and we all went to work with shovels. Travel in the Sahara without a shovel is like traveling in northern Norway without one! Of course on some of the remote roads between Norway and Sweden you have the extra fun of dealing with ice water and mud.

Fortunately the sandy area was not extensive. The sand had to be removed and the sand tracks laid down several times and the Germans were not only back on the track-they were down the track and out of sight—Again!

It is a frustrating experience to be so close to a village like Timimoun and not be able to spend some time there. Some fortunate people have the ability to return to such a place several times if they desire. We were not in that position. Ours was a once-in-a-lifetime journey through a small part of the Sahara. It was, and has been, our great loss to have had to travel so quickly past a village like Timimoun.

From our guide-books we had learned of the brick-red mud buildings studded with wooden spikes. It is said to be in a unique location with spectacular views over an ancient salt lake.

Another road-side camp was made just north of Adrar near a village named El-Kasabi. There were a few mud buildings and many, many children! Upon our arrival they were very curious. Emma had several bags of wrapped hard candy that they loved. She made them form a line which they did. However, as soon as they collected a piece of candy from the front they again joined the line at the rear! After some time Emma started to wave her finger at such tactics when repeated too frequently. They soon tired of the game and we were left alone.

Early the next morning everyone was up and moving about. Emma had fried eggs and potatoes for all. We all stood outside and ate, neither VW could seat five people. The German boys had no cooking facilities. We had no idea how, or what, they ate when Emma did not cook for all of us.

Along the track leading into Adrar we saw the fouggara. They mark the course of underground water channels. On the surface all one sees is a line of low wells. The channels into Adrar originally ran a distance of about 1500 miles! We were told that they were dug by hand, probably by slaves. The wells went down to the level of the water-table. The water was then carried up and ran in horizontal channels into the next well. It must have required a tremendous expenditure of human energy. The wells have now been replaced by modern pumps and pipes.

The next morning, our desert caravan pulled into the Great Square of Adrar surrounded by thick-walled red mud buildings. We parked in front of the Prefects office and the blazing sun was hot, Very hot! The area of the square was simply enormous! The red mud buildings surrounding the square were offices and business places.

The walls seemed to be about two feet thick, the doors and windows very small. The design was meant to keep out the intense desert heat. Picturesque low mud arches fronted the hotel and coffee shop. At night the dim light produced by a generator for a short time was swallowed up by the immensity of the giant square.

Adrar is based at an oasis. It is the source of life for the people and their agricultural produce. It is also an administrative center for Algeria's second-largest province. It is the location of several different cultures that date back hundreds of years. Each culture produces characteristic hand-crafts that are unique.

During the afternoon nothing moved. All human activity took place in the morning and late afternoon. After trying to move about in the square during the afternoon in the blazing hot sun the visitor very quickly adapts local customs. Emma had difficulty identifying the local grocery store and, when she did locate it, found very few items that she could use. Fortunately, she had an adequate supply of everything that we had to have.

From Adrar the main track went directly to Aoulef. If we had looked more closely at our maps we would have noticed that only a primitive track ran directly east from Reggan to Aoulef. Actually we loaded up with fuel and water in Adrar and set out for Reggan and on to Ain Salah. Just about everyone, except us, knew that Reggan is known as one of the hottest locations in the Sahara.

As usual, before leaving Adrar we checked our supplies—Especially water and fuel. If you do have a break-down in the desert it will require several days for the authorities to determine that you are really late in reporting at the next village. Then they have to send out a search party. They do not want to go to that trouble and expense unless there is good reason to think that you are in trouble. If you are at all desert-wise you will have plenty of water. Each person should have at least a gallon of water per day!

Satisfied that everything was in as much readiness as possible, we set off toward Reggan. Of course the Panzer Division disappeared down the sandy tract in minutes, we followed our compass almost due south. We were right on the edge of the famous Plateau De Tademait and we knew from our maps that Reggan was located just off the southern edge of the plateau. The vast flat-topped plateau extended for miles to out left, to the east and a sand sea, the Erg Czech, ran for many miles to our right, to the west. We were in little danger of losing our bearings on Reggan.

For some miles we actually traveled over the western edge of the plateau. It was very desolate and very flat! The track presented little in the way of scenery or problems. There were small villages to our west but, they were out of sight.

The Germans did not appear until we pulled into Reggan. How long would they have waited if we had failed to appear? We really did not know—But, we did wonder??

To the west of Reggan is Polisario territory. Since they have been known to take likely individuals as hostages, we did not consider thinking about traveling west of Adrar and Reggan. The Polisario Gorillas could have made the mistake of taking me hostage for money—How would they know that no one in the US would give anything in order to save my life? Their chances with Emma would have been much better!

When Emma passed out the hard candy, the Arab children called me Alli-Baba, probably because of my full beard. What would the Polisario think that Alli-Baba might bring them in the way of hard-cash? We did not want to find out!

Reggan was the site of the French A-Bomb tests in 1960-61. It is also the site of several natural gas wells. In time, the natural gas wells, and the possibility of finding oil would change that area of the Sahara far into the future. However, the Sahara is so vast that the sites of natural gas and oil wells, although they do alter the natural ecology of the local area, really have little effect upon the desert as a whole.

It was near Reggan that, in 1962' a French military patrol solved the mystery of the disappearance of an Australian Aviator in 1933. He had made several previous flights over the Sahara starting in the early 20s. On some of the flights he had a woman co-pilot but, on what would prove to be his last adventure, he was flying solo.

Flying a plane anywhere in 1933 was dangerous. Flying a plane across the Sahara at that time was far more than dangerous. The plan was to fly from England to South Africa! His plane went down near Reggan. After a search failed the incident went unnoticed into history. It was known that he went down somewhere on the Tademait Plateau. The plateau is desolate, even for the Sahara. Very few travelers attempt to cross such a flat, table-like, barren area.

The mystery was not solved until 1962. At that time a French Military patrol happened upon the wreckage of the lost plane. His mummified body was found under one wing of the plane where he sought relief from the scorching sun. On the plane he could not carry any appreciable volume of water. In any event he could never have survived in such a large uninhabited area.

His body was quite well mummified by the dry climate and intense sun. Still visible over one eye was a gash sustained when the plane crashed. The fact that his body was intact indicates that no animal life of any kind appeared to use it as a source of food. That would indicate the fact that the Tademait Plateau is devoid of any predators, scavengers, birds, or insects! The plateau has not changed over the years.

The adventurous Australian left a journal. His last entry stated his hope that someone would find the journal—and that help would arrive before it was too late!

The area around Reggan has another distinction—In February and March of 1961-62 the French held A-Bomb tests. To many of us that would be a very dubious distinction. The fact that the plateau might be one of the largest uninhabited areas in the world does not excuse or justify the insanity of such an act.

Not far from Reggan natural gas fields are being developed. That development will change the lives, and the economy of the area. Since the gas will be sold and piped to Europe, it will have far-reaching economic and political effects. Workers from the oases will be drawn away from agricultural labor by easier, and better-paying jobs in the gas and oil fields. Local food production will decline, prices will soar, and dependence upon foreign imports will increase. The self-sufficiency and independence of the oasis will be lost.

Reggan was hot, unbelievably hot! During the heat of the afternoon sun we sat under the thick walls of the low-arched entry to the coffee shop. When you tried to look out into the square the glare of the sun hurt your eyes. We never saw anyone walk across the square from late morning until late afternoon.

At coffee we were joined by an interesting couple. She was quite young and naïve. He was several years her senior. They had arrived in Reggan several days earlier riding on top of a loaded lorry. (truck) They had to have come from Benni-Abbes. We never did learn their point of origin and it did not seem wise to ask too many questions.

How did they manage to get past the Prefects in all the villages to the north? What was keeping them from starving? Where did they plan to go?

Their answers to questions were vague at best. They appeared tired, hungry, and very much in need of a bath and clean clothes. They did admit that they were under strict orders from the Prefect in Reggan to head north n the next passing lorry. Emma wanted to help them. So did I! But, we were in the southern Sahara, our funds were very limited, we not only had to get out of the desert, we had to get back across the Atlantic Ocean!

The Germans had to hold up for a few days in Reggan. They were waiting to hear from Germany. That, we guessed, indicated that they had resources of some kind back in Germany. It made us feel better about them.

One very hot afternoon (the only kind of afternoon that occurs in Reggan) we were parked in the shade of a palm tree. (I would not suggest planting palm trees for shade.) A lone figure could be seen slowly materializing out of the blazing heat being reflected from the hot, burning sand. To our disbelieving eyes it became a man carrying a sheep! He was in rags, bare-footed and bare-headed. In sign language he indicated that it was too hot for the animal to walk! After he left we all discussed what we had just witnessed and arrived at the conclusion that he must have been a slave.

The young men finally received their communication from Germany. We all checked, and double-checked our supplies of food, fuel, and water. We knew that we would face the most difficult section of track between Reggan and Ain Salah.

Early the following morning we set out east, toward Ain Salah. In the Sahara the prevailing wind blows from the north-east. The track from Reggan to Ain Salah runs, generally to the north-east. That meant that, in general, we would be traveling into the wind. As we traveled north-east the wind picked up. It carried the fine sand directly into our wind-screens. An eerie light was created and visibility quickly became very poor indeed. We knew that Ain Salah was almost directly to our east so, we kept a very close eye on the compass. The track frequently disappeared. When we were able to make out the tracks of lorries that had passed this way they went in all directions. Each driver created a new set of track! There were supposed to be, at intervals, visible gas cans called pylons. That or piles of stones. The cans were often knocked down, blown away, or taken by the Arabs for some other use. Under such conditions it was not possible to travel out of first or second gear. Very slow-going indeed! I worried that the wind-screen might become permanently pitted.

We have no idea how many hours we traveled in first gear. The fuel tank had to be filled! With that fine sand penetrating everything, it was going to be a dangerous procedure. I unlocked one six-gallon can from the rear, near the filler pipe. Emma did her best to screen the operation from the blowing sand. I quickly up-ended the can and emptied it. Neither of us said anything, we were both hoping that not enough sand got into the fuel to damage the motor. When the motor kicked over and we set off once more we both looked at each other and breathed a deep sigh of relief!

The morning passed, seemingly, very slowly. There was no mention of a stop for lunch. We were hoping that we would run out of the sand-storm or, that it would let up. Neither event happened.

It was very fortunate that we had an air-cooled motor. A normal-sized radiator almost surely would have boiled over. With the VW, the hotter it got, the better it ran! There were a couple other things in our favor. I had rigged up an over-sized oil filter and a fuel filter that could be dumped and cleaned with gasoline. Also, the oil filter did not require a cartridge—it was easy to wash out in gasoline, followed by a bath in motor oil.

It started to get dark. Where was the Panzer Division? With the light failing and the sand blowing, we were thinking of just stopping where we were—And hoping that a lorry would not come along and put an end to our Saharan Safari!

Suddenly Emma startled me with a sharp, excited shout! "Over there", she yelled, "What is that?" It was a very vague form of something, but the desert was perfectly barren and flat, nothing to be seen. I drove in that direction. There it was, the Panzer VW! The Germans were standing around looking at it. They had driven over a four foot rock ledge! Their battery had become loose and, when they went over the ledge, it turned upside-down. All the water had escaped! The VW would not start.

It was time for me to issue an order! "That is it for today. Maybe the storm will abate over-night. We will do what we have to do in the light of morning." We all went to bed and to sleep.

The morning sunrise was blood-red with a few scattered clouds on the horizon. The clouds vanished quickly and the hot sun quickly warmed the bone-chilling night air. By the time Emma fried the last of our eggs and some potatoes for the whole expeditionary desert force the Germans were anxious to get their vehicle started and extricated from its location at the base of the ledge.

There were two problems—1. Could the battery be saved? 2. How to get the VW away from the rock ledge and back onto the open track? First, the battery—I told Dieter that if all else failed we had a second battery that they could borrow until we reached Ain Salah where a new one could be purchased. I had wired in the second battery as a back-up for our water pump and lights. Since it was wired in parallel, we could easily remove it and get by on one battery.

Dieter did not like to take one of our batteries, he wanted to try to save his battery. So, I told him that we had some distilled water and a small bottle of battery acid. We could replace the lost water and take a guess at how much acid to add. The Germans liked that idea. The battery was filled, acid added, and this time it was wired down so that it could not come loose!

Now to get their VW out into the open and see if it would start? We each had long ropes intended for getting water out of deep wells. The ropes were folded back and forth and made in a toe-chain that reached from their VW to ours. We had to remain on the most firm sand if we were going to be able to pull them out. On the front of our vehicle we had mounted two new snow tires. The snow tires were partly deflated and put on the rear wheels of our VW.

Now we were as ready as we thought we could be. I was behind the wheel of our VW, Emma got behind the wheel of the stuck vehicle, and the three Germans got into position to push when I blew the horn. I blew the horn, let out the clutch, the snow tires dug into the loose sand and threw up quite a cloud! But they did take hold! Slowly the stranded VW came away from the ledge and up onto the track!

The next problem—Would it start? Dieter got in and we continued to pull their VW down the track—It started! The plan then was to let it run as long as possible but, in the event that it stalled or had to be turned off, say for the night, they would park so that we would be able to get behind them in order to push it. As we got started everyone had only one question in mind—Would their battery take a charge?

We continued to head just about due east toward Ain Salah. The topic was, not surprisingly, travel in the Sahara. Emma commented, "If we face such problems, what must it have been like when men such as Barth, Caillie, Richardson, Denham, Clapperton, Oudney, and hundreds of others tried to cross the Sahara in just about every possible direction?" "Each of those men wrote one or more books describing their travels through the Sahara," I answered. "Barth, the German compiled five volumes."

Barth had a classical education. He had the will and determination to succeed to match that education. In 1850 he set out on what was to be a 10,000 mile expedition through, and across the Sahara to Timbuktu. Throughout the journey he kept detailed notes relating to weather conditions, plants and animals, rock formations, as well as three temperature readings each day.

On one occasion Barth was lost in the desert for three days with one leafless tree for shade. He was eventually located but not before his raging thirst had forced him to attempt drinking his own blood! On another leg of the expedition he was forced, because of a sand storm to abandon several supply camels and an unknown number of slaves. Barth survived to reach a village and water. The five volumes that he finally published were so detailed and scientific that the public refused to read them. However, they proved to be invaluable to future explorers.

Rene Caillie was the first European to reach Timbuktu, (1820). He traveled disguised as a Muslim. While living in the village for almost a year he kept detailed notes on every aspect of daily life that became available to him. He also made accurate sketches of the buildings and some of the people. When his reports were published in Europe he was accused of fabricating them. Thirty years later, when Heinrich Barth finally made it to Timbuktu, he was able to verify what Caillie had sent back. When Caillie finally decided to leave Timbuktu with many of his reports and sketches he was murdered by a group of waiting Arabs a short distance from the village. He was beaten and stabbed. As he laid bleeding and dying the fanatic Arabs danced as they burned his work. The Sahara was, and still is, a very dangerous place!

The Dr. Oudney, Major Denham, Lieutenant Clapperton expedition set out from Tripoli for Lake Chad In 1822. They reported finding hundreds of parched, dried skeletons of men and camels. Denham reported that the bones crackled as his horse stepped on them and, in one instance, the horse kicked a human skull like a football.

In the 1800's Europeans knew almost nothing about the Sahara and/or Africa. The desert had been occupied for thousands of years. It had been crossed by Arab caravans for hundreds of years. But, to Europeans, it remained to be "discovered".

The expeditionary force labored onward toward Aoulet. This time the Panzer Division again took the lead, but not quite so fast and not quite so far ahead! We saw a few palm trees and a few scattered mud buildings that might have been stores or shops of some kind. We parked and the Germans went searching for a battery. They returned, as we expected, without one.

Since we were, at least, in a village and we had seen several other vehicles, we all had the same idea-or question. Two questions—Should we try it? Will it start? Dieter made the decision. He jumped behind the wheel and turned the key. It started! His breathless audience of four relaxed. But, we all had the next question in mind—Would the battery hold the charge?

In the morning we left Aoulet. The track ascended the edge of the Plateau Du Tademait. In places it was rather rough going. There were large jagged stones on the track that were best avoided. On the left the crumbling rock wall went straight up. On the right the soft bank of broken rock and sand went straight down. We would have had a great view—if there had been anything to look at! When we reached the edge of the plateau, just before the track went back down onto the sand, we happened upon a group of petrified trees.

The trees are well-known; the location is marked on our Michelin maps. We did not know that the track would pass close to them. The trees have been dated and thought to have grown some 100 million years ago. The trees fell into soft ground. The branches decayed but the large trunks absorbed silica carried by underground water. The silica and other minerals slowly replaced every molecule of the original living tree. The entire structure was entombed and turned to rock. After thousands, millions of years passed they were again slowly exposed by the erosive action of wind and water. Over eons of time the Sahara has passed through many wet and dry periods each lasting thousands of years. At times the Sahara has been tropical. At other times it has been much dryer and much larger then it is at present.

Over the past million years primitive men have occupied the desert during wet periods. They moved in to hunt animals such as are now found in East Africa. As the desert went into a dry period the animals died off and the hunters either moved out or died with them. At the present time the Sahara is in a dry period. It is moving south at several miles each year. Part of the expansion is, no doubt, due to natural climate change. However, it is being augmented by the over-population of people, agriculture, and herding practices. Global warming is another major player. The prognosis for the Sahara, and for the planet, is not good.

There was evidence of life in, and around, the tree trunks. I saw the tracks of mice, birds, and insects. There must have been activity on cloudy days, and during the evening, night, and early morning. Emma and I wanted to stay and make camp. The Germans, worried about their battery wanted to get on toward Ain Salah. We thought to ourselves that they could worry about the battery here on top of the plateau or down at the base of it—What would be the difference?

We made our way down the track from the plateau and back out onto the sand. The difference between the track going up and the one coming down was only that the track down was shorter! Once we were down off the plateau we had to camp.

We decided that the following day would put us in Ain Salah—That is, if we did not run into any unforeseen problems!

But, we did run into problems! The first was that the wind came up again and the sand started to blow. The Germans had used a good part of the day in Aoulef trying to locate a new battery. Now the light was starting to fade and the sand blowing reduced visibility to a few feet. We could make out the track and, with the compass we knew that we were headed in about the right direction for Ain Salah.

East of Aoulef, at a brief stop to be sure we were on the track, we convinced the Germans that we would have to make one more camp before Ain Salah. We knew that, had they been alone, they would have tried to make it. We convinced them that we were older and tired more easily. They were considerate. We all realized that it would be too dangerous to park for the night on, or even close to, the track. The Arab lorry drivers make desert driving simple, they floor the accelerator, let out the clutch, and aim the vehicle in the desired direction!

We slowly went over a slight rise. I was concentrating on the track and keeping the Panzer vehicle in view. The sand storm was so bad that it slowed the Germans to a first gear crawl. As we came over the rise Emma said, "Look at all those stones sticking up out of the sand". We stopped. There were not stone outcrops or ledges marked on our maps. Close investigation revealed the most forsaken, desolate, cemetery imaginable! The sand blowing, the dim fading light. The utter desolation of the setting actually was most depressing.

Any obstruction in the path of wind-blown sand will start the formation of a sand dune. Each grave, was marked by a plain jagged stone, started the formation of a small dune on the leeward side. Although I tried to take some pictures, they failed completely to capture the abandonment and complete desolation of that cemetery along the sandy track in the Sahara.

Off to our right the dim outline of some one-story, mud-brick buildings at the end of a short side track came into view. The appearance and mood created by that village in the midst of a raging sand storm, after just passing the cemetery, could not have been more depressing, especially when you add to the mix the fact that we had been traveling for many hours and, in the storm could not be certain of our location.

There were no signs; we did not expect to see any. We tried to guess where we might be on our maps. According to the maps and the distance we had traveled from Reggan we thought we might be in a village called "Tit". We also could have been in a place name "In-Rhar".

Huge sand dunes surrounded the low mud buildings. From what we were able to make out it would be just a matter of years before some of them would be covered! We drove into what might have been the main street. It was a wide sandy expanse between two rows of low buildings. For an instant the area as far as we could see in the glare of our headlights, was vacant. Suddenly the two vehicles were completely surrounded by a mob of adults and children. Everyone that I could make out was dressed in tattered, torn, soiled rags. I do not remember seeing one piece of solid clothing. All the children were holding their hands out, begging and screaming.

Dieter made his way back to my window. "No one understands German, French, or English," he said. "We can not camp here. We will have to drive down the track a few miles and just try to get out of the way". I agreed. Emma was throwing hard candy out by the hands full! The crowd, the screaming and yelling intensified. I tried to stay calm on the surface but, at that moment I was very nervous. In truth, I was scared as hell! I do not think that they meant us any harm. If only even one of us could have communicated with someone the situation would not have seemed so threatening. As we slowly pulled away many of the children tried to hold onto the camper. I could see them through the rear-view mirror trying to cling to the jerry cans attached in the back to each side. As we gained momentum they gave up.

Traveling through foreign countries is a wonderful experience. It is much more rewarding if you are able to exchange ideas with the natives. In all our travels we have keenly felt that a great deal of interesting information was missed because we could not speak the native language. Esperanto, the international language based upon all the major languages, was a great idea, we thought. Obviously the majority of people on the planet did not agree.

The sand-blown wind did not slacken until daybreak. Emma had some eggs left and some dried ham or salami, whatever, she made breakfast sand witches for all. We stood outside trying to talk to each other through Dieter. The conversation revolved around Ain Salah. How far did we have to go? What might we encounter before getting there? Each one of us had different ideas. No one really knew.

Again the track was a real challenge to negotiate. There were many very sandy areas and some soft spots. I was certain that the Germans would find their way into one. I was wrong! They slowed down and selected the firm sand every time. The truth is that I relaxed, a little, and tended to rely on their judgment.

A few miles from Ain Salah we encountered a barrier that not even the Panzer Division could negotiate! It was not the track. Compared to what we had just been over, the track was in very good condition. It was a sand dune about ten feet high! Everybody bailed out to check the dune. We all climbed to the top and tried to find a way around it. We located the track on the other side but, that was of no help.

Finally one of the Germans found a faded sign lying by the side of the dune. As best we could make out it had a barely visible red arrow which, we guessed, if the sign were held upright and parallel with the dune, pointed north. We headed north, keeping the dune to our right. When the slip-face of the dune was reached we drove around it and headed back south to get back on the track, (The slip-face is the direction in which the dune is traveling. The sand is carried by the prevailing wind up the gentle slope on the windward side and then falls sharply forming a steep bank.)

After getting around the dune and finding the main track into Ain Salah we all felt that, at last, we had made it. Not so!

The track was very narrow and sandy. As it entered a thick grove of beautiful Palm trees, we were brought to a sudden halt by a huge vehicle parked squarely in the track! As we all exited our vehicles to determine what might be wrong, the occupants of the sand-tractor hauled out a large cooler. The cooler was placed in the middle of the track, in the welcome shade of the palms.

When it was opened it was found to be packed with beer, soda, and ice! The men were French desert, oil prospectors on "leave" to Ain Salah. Of course they knew the Prefect in Ain Salah and they knew by radio messages about when we should arrive. They had driven out to be sure that we did not go the wrong way around the dune. I checked the map—That would not have been a good idea!

Everyone was tired, hot, and thirsty. The Germans were very thirsty! As we all tried our best to empty the cooler we talked. We wondered why the French would be prospecting for oil in the Sahara just after years of fighting. They explained that although the war of independence was long and bitter, the French still managed to leave on relatively friendly terms. One man said, "It is the Americans that the Algerians hate. They will not allow American prospectors into the desert." "That is why the Americans pay us to do the prospecting." "The Americans pay you?" "Yes, they pay for everything! They are paying for the beer and soda that you are drinking; they pay for our vehicles and the fully-equipped living quarters in which we live when out in the desert. The Americans pay for everything."

I do not know what the Germans thought, they made no comment. I fell silent. I thought, "That is typical US foreign policy. We throw money at every problem and everyone on the planet hates us for it."

The conversation turned to lighter topics. The problem of the sand dunes encroaching upon the houses in Ain Salah, the water problems, the over-population, and the exodus of agricultural labor to better-paying jobs in the near-by oil fields. We were to learn more about the old, and the new, problems facing an oasis that had existed through many good and hard times over the past hundreds of years.

The daylight began to fade; the cooler went empty and the wonderful, thoughtful desert party thrown by the French, and the Americans, ended with handshakes all around. It was great! We went looking for the only hotel in Ain Salah in a very happy mood!

The architecture, the style of the hotel blended perfectly with the desert atmosphere. Even I could determine that, at one time, it was a most pleasant place to rest after crossing the Sahara. Time and human nature change everything. Politics determined that the management of the hotel must pass into the hands of the Arabs. The paint was peeling; the walled-in front yard was unkempt, only the bar seemed to be functioning. The only safe drink served was beer. That was the only thing that most of us wanted!

During the day we all went our own way exploring the oasis. There were thousands of date palms. To be more exact 225,000 of them! There were thousands of potential desert pictures presented. The narrow tracks with mud-walls and stately tall palms along each side were very picturesque to us. Many blacks were laboring throughout the oasis tending the palms, fruit trees, and vegetable gardens. The irrigation system required constant, back-breaking manual labor.

It was hot! Ain Salah is at an elevation of 275 meters. (1 meter equals about one yard.) Blacks, wearing only ragged loin-cloths labored in the burning sun. They dug irrigation channels with wide-bladed hoes by hand, and then hauled in mud that they had loaded into baskets, one on each side of a burrow. The mud was dumped and packed along the water-ways in an attempt to make them more impervious.

As we watched Emma said, "Slavery is said to have been outlawed in most countries of the world." We spent some time watching and talking. Yes, slavery may be illegal, But, suppose that you are born in the middle of the Sahara and have absolutely no education. You have no money and no knowledge of the world outside of the oasis.

Where would you go? What could you possibly do? Easy to say, "Get out, go someplace else." Keep in mind that you barely are able to communicate in the local dialect; you have no money, and, no clothes! By the standards of those laboring blacks we were very wealthy. We had clothes, shoes, food, water, transportation, and money! Give it some serious though. Once you are down, really down, it is very difficult to get up.

What did we do? After spending the afternoon watching that scene we returned to the hotel, met the Germans on their way to the bar and, joined them. We did not even try to discuss the situation with them; they were too young and, just not concerned about the internal affairs of Algeria. They were quite right in having that attitude. We had learned that fact the hard way in Tunisia many years ago.

Every night that we gathered in the bar to drink bottled beer and discuss, at great length, matters of no importance, The Prefect of Ain Salah sat quietly in a corner where he could see and hear everything that transpired. It was his responsibility to know everything that was taking place under his jurisdiction. Some time later, when we had an encounter with one of his young, hot-headed, underlings, we were very pleased that the Prefect had been there and that he realized we were simple travelers.

One day two young graduate students from the University of California pulled in. They were driving an over-loaded, late-model VW. They were doing Graduate Work in Mammology, collecting small mammals, such as desert mice, as part of a study relating to population and ecology. Their vehicle was so over-loaded that they were forced to sleep outside, on the ground, in sleeping bags. The remainder of the day was spent listening to their experiences out in the desert.

They would select a likely looking habitat, and then set up camp. The traps were set in the evening before dark. Most small animal activity has to take place after the sun sets. The only way they could survive and reproduce would be to escape the heat of the day. At night food must be located, and then, perhaps, a mate. It is a dangerous game of eating and, avoiding being eaten. Some animals hide in caves, under rock ledges, or dig burrows. Desert owls prefer finding abandoned burrows. Insects, and scorpions, as well as snakes, horned viper rattlers, burrow into the sand.

The students frequently had difficulty explaining their strange behavior to passing Arab tribesmen, and to local authorities. A great help was official permission to trap and collect written in Arabic. That helped when the Arabs were able to read.

One evening they returned after about three days out in the desert. They were hungry, tired, thirsty, and rather badly burned. Since the Germans had departed south toward the southern Sahara, Emma took it upon herself to take care of them.

Water came first. Then she had sunburn cream for their faces and arms. That was followed by sandwiches for all. (Even me) After the sandwiches were devoured, they regained enough strength to walk over to the hotel bar. As far as we could determine, the water did very little to quench their thirst! The Prefect sat in the corner as usual. Following our bout at the bar we all returned to our respective vehicles. Emma made up our bed in the camper and the students spread out their tarps and sleeping bags. There was not a sound to be heard until morning.

The next evening, when we returned from visits to the artesian wells and the diesel-driven deep well pumps we found two more VW campers. Two couples were attempting to cross the desert, this time to Nigeria. We were told that, even with a proper Nigerian visa, people had made it to the border and been turned away. If that information had any effect upon them, it was not obvious.

The one VW had a generator problem. (Generator, not alternator.) The other German was making new brushes. How he was able to do it we never learned. From that we thought that, if anyone could get on across to Nigeria, they probably could. We were not as certain about the German Panzer Division making it.

Once again Emma's charges returned from a collecting foray in the desert. This time they were not interested in food, they wanted to visit the bar. They were young and, we could tell, not experienced beer-drinkers. As the evening passed the bar became rather cluttered with empty beer bottles. It also became obvious that the students had taken on a little more than they might be able to manage. Emma, who drank very little, finally managed to convince all of us that it was time to return to the camper.

Since her charges had not eaten Emma felt that she should feed them. First, she made strong black coffee. I could not see that it was having the desired effect. Then she decided that we all should have sandwiches. The one student managed to get the food down and keep it there. All four of us were crowded around our small table in the VW. It was impossible to get in and out in a hurry, even if you were sober. For the one student it turned out to be impossible!

Emma took charge. She cleaned him up and got him back outside, got his sleeping bag out and got him into it. Then we cleaned up the camper so that we could get to bed. No one had any difficulty sleeping that night!

The following day was a quiet one. We were all trying to recover from the events of the previous night. The graduate students were content to just sit around discussing the problems that life faces in the desert. They were impressed by the many evolutionary adaptations exhibited by any form of life that has managed to survive under some of the most hostile conditions on the planet.

The major problem is water. Just as important is the ability to get rid of excess heat. A few animals, like the camel, are able to store limited amounts of water. Water is also stored in the form of fat. Some water can be extracted from the fat when it is burned. The camel's long neck, legs, and abdomen serve to radiate excess heat. Also, the long legs of the camel raise the bulk of the body up from the surface of the sand. That can mean a lowering of the temperature as much as 25 degrees The long legs of the ostrich serve the same function. The long neck of the ostrich also radiates heat. The small jerboa has big, long, wide ears that provide a large radiating surface. Many of the small mammals get the water that they require from the plants that they eat. They are able to extract water from their food, called metabolic water. Some large animals the size of a gazelle have thick coats that serve to protect them. They are able to allow their body temperature to rise during the heat of the day and, radiate it into the atmosphere during the night.

Predators, such as the small cat-sized fennec (Saharan fox) extract the water required from their prey. The fennec also has large ears through which it radiates heat. Gazelle, gemsbok, addax, and the ibex sweat. The zebra that invades the edge of the desert on occasion also sweats. Birds in the desert are often capable of making flights to water sources. The turtle dove is reported as flying fifty miles in order to secure the free water that it requires daily. Most birds drink by filling their beaks and letting the water run down their throats. Doves drink like human being; they suck in the water and swallow it. When they return to the nest they regurgitate the water if stimulated by the young inserting their beaks down the throat of the adult. If the chick is young, it gets pigeon milk from the crop, if it is older, it gets water. The African sand grouse flies to water each morning. They have a unique way of carrying water to their young. While drinking they immerse their breast feathers in the water. The feathers absorb water like a sponge. When the adult returns to the nest the young extract the water from the feathers with their beaks. Some birds, during the heat of the day, seek shade under a rock ledge and engage irregular panting or rapid throat fluttering. The evaporation of water from their throat membranes helps to radiate heat. Reptiles, and some beetles, are able to escape the heat by burrowing into the sand. The temperature of the sand might be 165 degrees Fahrenheit, one yard above the surface the temp would be about 122 F. Two yards above the surface, where the bulk of a camels body would be, the temp. of 110 should be expected. About one yard below the surface the temp. would be between 86 and 90 F.

If a snake, bird, or insect can manage to climb into a bush or tree it has a good chance of avoiding a lethal temperature. The same is true with respect to any animal able to burrow beneath the surface or use the burrow created by some other creature.

The evolutionary adaptations of desert plants would require a separate book, or books. Desert ecology is far more complex than most people realize. That is why it was so frustrating to Emma and I to have to travel across such a large section of the desert in convoy, but, it was that way or no way!

Hawks, eagles, and vultures soar above the desert at heights of about 300 yards. In that region the average temp. would be 79 F. The daily fluctuation in temperature at the surface of the sand is the most extreme of that in any natural habitat. The same can be said with respect to the variation in humidity.

There is a desert beetle, one of many, that lives in the sand to escape the lethal surface temps. Early in the morning it rises to the surface, raises its posterior end and almost stands on its head. In that position any moisture that might be in the air would condense on the surface of the beetle's body and trickle down toward the anterior end for the beetle to drink.

Another interesting evolutionary adaptation to desert life is that of certain ants. These "honey-pot" ants form a special caste known as "repletes". During times when moisture and food are in abundance, the workers fill the crops of the repletes with liquid carbohydrates. The crops become so distended that the honey-pot ant or replete is barely able to move. They attach themselves to the roof of a chamber and serve as food reserves. Any hungry ant can approach a honey-pot and, by gently stroking its antenna, secure a tiny drop of liquid food. A nest might contain more than one thousand repletes.

The desert nomads, such as the Tuareg who live in the mountains in the south know about the honey-pot ants. In time of scarcity they raid the nests and steal the highly nutritious food stored there.

The Tuareg are an interesting tribe. They inhabit the southern Sahara Mountains. For many years the Tuareg were able to control the trade routes crossing the Sahara. They had a reputation established by raiding and looting caravans that failed to pay them tribute. In the past a large amount of material moved across the Sahara from the east and from the south. Everything moved on the backs of camels, and slaves. It is estimated that the camel has been used in the Sahara for about the last one thousand years.

The amount of material moved and the animal and human energy expended would be impossible to estimate. Some of the caravans required hundreds of camels, traders, free-men, and slaves. Thousands of slaves were captured or purchased from African Chiefs or black, local raiders in West, and Central Africa.

Many of the slaves moved through Ain Salah because the Arabs were in control of the trade in, and around, AinSalah. However, the Tuareg were firmly in control of the trade routes in the southern Sahara. Slave auctions were regularly held in a market building in central Ain Salah. The building still stands and is presently used on a daily basis. Plenty of fresh vegetables, fruit, dates, and several kinds of meat are for sale. Usually it is necessary to shoo the flies away in order to determine the kind of meat being offered.

Emma did her daily shopping in that former slave-trading building. It had a sturdy-looking roof with large supporting columns. It was open on all sides and anyone who had anything to offer for sale or trade was free to use it. Many did, mostly women. Beautiful jewelry, made by the Tuareg was offered and Emma was very tempted. She did buy one outstanding clasp that had been used to hold the rather voluminous blue shawls worn by the Tuareg.

We frequently saw Tuareg tribesmen shopping in the market-place. They rode in on big, beautiful, stately white camels. Their blankets and saddles, with the rather large cross standing out, were conspicuous. We never saw more that two Tuareg men in the market at the same time. They would appear, seemingly out of nowhere, completely covered by yards of blue-dyed flowing cloth. Their heads and faces were always completely covered, only a narrow slit remained open through which they could see. A loose Vail hung down over their noses and mouths. We were told by a local Arab traveler who said that he had lived with a Tuareg family for short periods of time that the men never remove the veil in the presence of strangers. And, you are a stranger if you are not a family member. He said that when they eat they raise the veil just enough to place the food or drink into their mouths.

In the market they would dismount, transact their business very briefly, and ride out. It was surprising to us, the complete control they had over their mounts. They would appear, ride up; the camel would kneel down, front legs first, in seconds they were in the market. They were served instantly! Conversation with the traders was held to a minimum.

It was apparent that they were born and raised to be the masters. The Tuareg Masters led lives of relative ease and comfort. Their vassals or slaves did all the work. Recent events are changing the social structure of the Tuareg society, perhaps its very existence. The movement against slavery did not have any immediate effect upon the practice in the Sahara, but very slowly, over the years, it has made it less rampant. Some Arab countries have been very slow in making the transition to a society in which all human beings have relative freedom.

Events in Europe had more of an effect in the Sahara. As early as the sixteenth century large sailing ships were developed capable of carrying cargo far exceeding that of camels. With more accurate methods of navigation such vessels could sail around the Sahara and avoid all the perils of the dessert and the Tuareg tribesmen. More trade could be accomplished more efficiently. This was a blow to be felt by the Tuareg more and more as the years passed.

Recent events have been more devastating. An increase in car and truck transport has made transport by camel less necessary, less efficient. The diesel engine has had a devastating effect. With the increase in the reliability of vehicles has gone an increase in tourism. It is a proven fact that nothing is more destructive to a native society than an influx of tourists. Tourists are destroying the very things that they travel great distances to see. In the Sahara, tourists, with the ever-present camera are photographing.

Then there is the prolonged drought. This could be the final blow to the traditional way of life of the Tuareg. Former slaves tended the sheep and goats owned by their Tuareg masters. They moved the herds from one water source to another with the seasons. Now the desert is drying out and moving south. When the Tuareg move south they encounter Africans who already occupy the land. It is the ever-present population problem and, it is going to get worse!

Before the French invaded North Africa in their gallant effort to "save" the Arabs, the Tuareg controlled most of the Sahara. They controlled the caravan routes, moved with the seasons around the desert and through the mountains. Eventually, the French, in their superior and infinite wisdom, drew lines on their maps and created several countries, using the Sahara and other parts of west Africa. No consideration was given to the local tribes, especially the nomads. Those completely meaningless lines on the map created obstacles, and conflicts, that are today the source of insoluble problems. The recent discovery of minerals, gas, and oil, have compounded the problems and led to armed conflicts and the deaths of thousands of innocent local inhabitants.

Not only the French, several other advanced" countries took it upon themselves to invade, plunder, and "save", the Africans. Much of the damage was done by colonial officials and colonists. And, any part of native culture that they failed to destroy was finished off by the invading missionaries!

Following the withdrawals of the colonials and their mischief-making, the United States mounted an all-out effort to "free" the Black Man. The result of that costly effort has been the creation of constant local tribal wars and dictatorships in each country coerced or forced, to accept democracy."

What could be the final blow—The gas and oil wells! They occupy a relatively small area, but, they are having a profound effect! Little, if any of the wealth is getting down to the level of the average person. The effect upon the Tuareg way of life is due to the fact that opportunities for jobs in the gas and oil fields become available.

The gas and oil field jobs make it possible for some of the former Taureg vassals or slaves to make more money as laborers than they ever could have imagined. It would have required a lot more time, effort, money, and ability than we had to even begin to assess the desirable and undesirable effects created by development of the fields. We did learn one effect—The creation of a state of war in the Western Sahara and the formation of rebel opposition forces with the goal of destroying the present government, and the tourist trade.

Emma and I stayed away from the Western Sahara because of the Polisaro affair in which Morocco and Algeria were, and are involved. The north is best avoided because of so-called guerrilla attacks, shootings, and bombings. The south-east is not safe due to the possibility of being taken as a hostage and held for ransom. Emma's family would do anything possible to free her—I am quite certain that I would be on my own!

After a day at the former slave market it was back to the hotel and our evening meal—Stew! Emma made enough for the graduate students and we all sat on the ground and scooped it up. Each day we all went our separate ways. During the evening there was usually a discussion of what had been seen, and what we thought of it. After the evening meal it was time to retire to the hotel for refreshments.

There is something new to see and investigate every day in any oasis. We could have spent a month or more in Ain Salah but we did not have a month. The summer heat was beginning to start. Each day it got hotter and we had to travel over the Plateau Du Tademait on our way out. That stretch of track, while not as rough as what we had covered, was well known to be difficult.

Tamanrasset, south of Ain Salah, was one of our major objectives. At the pace we traveled it would have required another month. It was just impossible to try. We had spent too much time crossing Morocco. That, we did not regret. The trip should have been planned more carefully. A great deal was missed forever.

One day, while checking over the camper, I discovered that I had lost the wrench for the transmission. It would be impossible to check the fluid level without that wrench. And, no matter which way we decided to go from Ain Salah that definitely should be done. While I was checking the transmission I discovered that several of the bolts had come loose! I should have thought of that when we passed several abandoned vehicles along the tracks.

If you break down along a difficult section of track it can be very expensive to have your vehicle towed out for repair. Some people worked out a solution to that problem. They had the vehicle covered by insurance then, when they found that it would be too expensive to tow it out, they set fire to it! That worked for several years—That is until the insurance companies realized what was going on.

It was absolutely necessary that we get the trans. Open and check it. There was an open-air repair shop on the edge of the village. The mechanic, while he was unable to speak English, was quite able to think in Arabic.

When he emerged from under the camper he smiled and gestured. He was saying, "No problem."

He found a piece of old, rusty, scrap iron and a nut that fit the trans, fitting. In minutes he welded the nut to the end of the strip of scrap iron and, with a smile, handed me a new" trans. Wrench! When we offered to pay for it, he waved us off. Had he wanted to, he could have collected several US dollars for that wrench. We still have it—It is not for sale.

We did have a small container of trans, fluid. We used all of it! After the bolts were properly tightened we had no further difficulty in that department. The following day it was necessary that the irrigation system in the oasis be inspected. I also wanted to get some close-up pictures of a camel. What was not noticed at any time during our exploration of the oasis was that we were under surveillance!

The irrigation system was extensive, water ran through hand-made channels in all directions. The source of water was supplied by artesian wells and big diesel pumps. We were informed several times that Russia supplied the pumps and dug the wells. When the population was small the artesian well supplied an adequate amount of water. The recent estimate of the population is 35,000. That is a large number of people and they require more and more water.

When we asked about the level of the aquifer and if it was known how fast it might be falling, the answers were very vague. One man who spoke some English seemed to be saying that the water would be supplied by, "the mountains." He gestured that the water flowed from the mountains through underground rivers. I thought, That source of water could be erratic, limited, and undependable.

He probably had the Hoggar Mountains in mind. They are massive areas of jumbled, rock, stone, and high peaks located to the south of Ain Salah. There are many guelettas, or permanent pools located in those mountains. A surprising variety of plants and animals are dependent upon those pools of water. The last crocodile was shot in one of those ponds in the mid-eighteen hundreds! The traces of ancient Mediterranean flora and fauna found there today was stranded when the Sahara became hotter and expanded.

Ain Salah is doing the same thing that the Americans are doing in the west, pumping the water from aquifers that it has taken thousands of years to fill. The US might be able to get water from Canada. (They Might!) But from whom, from where, might Ain Salah be able to get water?

The irrigation system requires constant repair. The only men we saw digging and patching the channels were black. When we approached them they moved away. They either could not, or would not, attempt to talk with us. The language barrier was almost always with us!

We left the irrigation system and went looking for a camel that we might be able to photograph. We wanted to get some close-up shots. It was necessary to find a man with a camel who was not busy. We did not find one that day, but we did the following morning.

Since the camel was introduced into the Sahara from the east about two thousand years ago, it has gained a place prominence in Arab life and culture. It has been used as a beast of burden for moving just about everything. It is vital with respect to travel into, and through, desolate, remote areas. The urine is used as an antiseptic. The hide is used as a source of cloth, clothing, and shelter. Camels are milked, and finally consumed as food.

Camels are forever grumbling about something—Not that they do not have very good reasons! Emma made the comment that, in our brief association with camels, she never saw a "happy camel."

While walking along a sandy track between weathered mud walls and towering palms, a likely-looking subject appeared. Both he and the camel appeared to have seen better days. He stopped, wondering what it was that we wanted to do. Using a lot of sign-language, pointing and gesturing, it dawned upon him that it was his camel we wanted to photograph. I am quite certain that he thought it very odd that anyone would want to do that.

The camel was as cooperative as the owner. Emma and I were impressed by the appearance of both man and animal. As I photographed the head, eyes, ears, lips, etc., of the animal we were discussing the amount that we should offer the man. He first Laughed and refused the money, then accepted with a gesture of thanks.

At that moment the proceedings were interrupted by a thin young man who was very neatly dressed in a dark suit. He spoke English clearly. First he identified himself as some type of official agent. Then he went on, "You stay in Ain Salah a long time. You travel about and take many pictures. Please come with me."

He walked ahead leading us to a large mud building which we recognized as police headquarters and the office of the Prefecture. The Prefecture was not in so he started to explain the situation to several other officials. Everyone seemed to listen intently and we wondered what was happening and what was going to happen.

At that moment the Prefecture entered. It was obvious that he had heard about what was taking place and he obviously was displeased. He spoke clearly and sharply to the young man who had brought us in. We noticed that no one interrupted him. When he finished he turned to us and, throwing up he hands as if in disgust said, "Savau." He smiled a very thin smile and motioned that we were free to leave. Our exit was swift.

It was a good thing that it happened. We were feeling too much at home in a country that was becoming more paranoid by the day. The government was trying to solve current problems as well as those left by the former French occupation. Shootings and bombings were frequent in the north. Hostages were being taken in the southeast by rebel groups. There were serious problems with respect to the proper use and distribution of the recent gas and oil money. And, to add to the confusion there was, and is, the rampant growth of the population! Unemployment and poverty increased faster than the gas and oil money could be used to solve them. There was inadequate housing and trouble with the Berber tribes. Government officials were frustrated.

Now, (2008), it is not permitted to travel in Algeria without a licensed guide in your vehicle at all times. That would make wandering about freely in the Sahara the way we did impossible. We secured information from travelers who had camped, and lived with the Tuareg in the Hoggar Mountains. Under present restrictions on freedom of Movement we would not consider going to Algeria.

The United States has been demanding freedom for everyone around the world. That may sound like a noble cause. The trouble is that, in Africa, it has not worked! From Egypt to South Africa, freedom, and democracy simply do not exist.

A round-table strategy meeting of two was hastily convened that evening! A glance at our maps clearly indicated that we would have to make it across the Plateau De Tademait before reaching the oasis of El Golea. The sun was getting hotter every day; the plateau was flat, stony, and completely free of vegetation or animal life. And that included people! The decision was made to take one more day to check our food, water, fuel, and the motor of the camper. Then it would be an early start and the rough climb up the escarpment and out onto the plateau—This time alone!

As the sun rose we said good-bye to our friends and headed up the escarpment and onto the plateau. The track was mixed sand and stone. Some of the stones were quite large, better to go around them! The track had been cut into the side of the mountain and there was no guard rail. We never saw anything that looked like a guard rail in the Sahara. Once out on the plateau it was almost as flat as the top of a table. And, as we had been told, no sign of life, plant or animal. I do not remember seeing any birds.

As the day wore on the sun got hotter and the wind, laden with sand, started to blow. By the time we had to stop for lunch the intense heat defied description. We realized that we had spent too much time in Ain Salah. Well, actually, better planning was the problem. The proper time to get into the Sahara would be late October or early November, as soon as the heat starts to let up.

Emma spotted a barren, leafless tree. I pulled off the track toward it and stopped. The hot, sand-laden wind did nothing to alleviate the heat. The heat in the camper forced us to seek relief under the tree for lunch. The heat, wind, and sand blowing forced us to abandon the lunch idea and keep moving. I did not mention it but, the temperature in the motor compartment was very much on my mind. Remember? I mentioned that, with an air-cooled motor, the hotter it gets, the better it runs? "Well", I thought, "This is the ultimate test!" The VW never skipped a beat!

We did not think that it would ever happen—but, it did. The sun set and sank below the most desolate and barren place we had ever been. The only other place that might compare with the desolation that we could think of was Norway, well north of the Arctic Circle. There the problems were just the opposite—Snow, ice, mud, and cold!

Believe it or not, Emma said, "We have to do the laundry." Note that she said, "We." For that we had to rise before daylight. A large metal container normally used as the toilet had to be pressed into service. The water and soap were added and the lid sealed with clamps. As we traveled over the rough track the clothes were sloshed about as they are in an automatic washer. Next, Emma, started the rinse cycle.

On down the track I saw a large jagged rock. I pulled over close to it. A line was run from the camper and fastened around the rock. The desert does have advantages—during the summer they are few indeed, I admit. If you start to hang the clothes at one end of the line, by the time you reach the other end, the first ones are dry!

Being caught in the desert without plenty of water would be a fate that it is impossible to imagine! No wonder that the explorer, Barth, after three days, tried to drink his own blood! Having read about Barth, we carried three six-gallon cans of water. Yes, it was hot water, but that did not matter.

On the third day out we knew that we were near a village called Taboloulet. It was some distance off the track and at quite an elevation. We thought that it would make a good rest-stop. The Michelin map was right again! It was quite high up and the track leading up to it was even worse that that out of Ain Salah and up onto the Plateau.

It was not a village, it was a hotel. It was a rest-stop but it was closed for the summer. We did not wonder why.) A waiter was there, probably to keep the place from being robbed. He spoke English, and he made a pot of tea and found some biscuits. The hotel was closed so it would have been impossible to stay there. Anyway we wanted to stop at an old fort named "Miribel" and then on to El Golea. During our conversation he told us one important fact, he said, "You have stayed too late in the desert." Well, was just full of valuable advice—We had not thought of that!

The drive back down to the main track seemed more dangerous than the climb up. Emma was on the outside seat and, in several places the road had eroded away. She could look straight down the crumbling mountain to the valley several thousand feet below. She suggested that I keep more to the left, but on the left the mountain continued straight up—There was no "left"!

Back on the track we were headed north once more toward Fort Mirabel, an abandoned French garrison post used to keep the natives in check when they got restless, which was quite often.

Maybe I was too tired, too hot, too much in a hurry to get on north and away from the heat. I have used all those reasons for the mistake I made. I simply failed to see a large patch of soft sand! Before we knew what had happened the VW was buried up to the hubcaps! It is not difficult to see soft sand patches—but, you have to be alert! You have to know when you are out of the desert. I really was disgusted with myself. I wanted to be able to say that I drove from Bechar to Ain Salah and up to El Golea and back over to Figuig without getting stuck in the sand. Well, I can not say that.

No question that I had failed to do a fine job of it. We were buried. It would have taken hours of digging to remove the sand and use sand tracks even if we had them. The best thing to do was to stay with the vehicle and wait for another vehicle to come along, one with enough power to pull us out.

It can be lethal to lose your cool in the desert. The incident back in Ain Salah with the young paranoid official did un-nerve me. I did not think of telling the Prefecture that we were leaving, headed for El Golea. That meant that no one would look for us.

There was little danger, as long as we would be able to stand the heat. Both of us were young enough, and in fairly good physical condition. Our food and water supplies were more than adequate. Except for the heat we were prepared to hold out for a week or more if we were careful with the food. Emma checked the food and prepared to cut back just in case we did have a long wait.

The wait was not that long. But it did seem a very long time in that blast-furnace called the Sahara! The day wore slowly on—and on. We talked about the sun setting and how much cooler it would be. Neither of us had any appetite, but we did drink a lot of hot water.

The first day passed, eventually. Nothing moved on the track. It was too far and, too hot to attempt to walk back to the hotel up that mountain. We decided to wait it out in the camper. Our indoor thermometer went up to 123 F!! We sat across from each other and did not attempt to move or talk.

The second day passed. It was exactly the same as the first except that it seemed hotter. We did not look at the thermometer. As you sweat and the water evaporates almost instantly the wind-blown sand sticks to your skin. If you have any mental or physical defects that desert heat will amplify them. The heat of the day contrasted sharply with the cold of the night. Almost as soon as the sun set all the heat built up during the day radiated into the cloudless sky. The stars were brighter that we had ever seen. We even joked a little about that. In Texas they claim that the stars are "Big and Bright". Yes, they are—But not as bright as they are in the Sahara!

And the moon! Never did we see anything like it! When that huge yellow moon rises over the desert you even (almost) forget about the heat of the day and you are happy to be there and see it. But it does get cold! Not long after sun set we made up the bed and got into the double sleeping bags. That is we got into them after a sponge-bath.

How do I describe two people taking a sponge-bath in a VW camper? Emma suggests that I describe the procedure as briefly as possible. (I think that she really would prefer, not at all.)

It goes something like this: One person sits in the front. The other one fills the sink with water. First the body part is made wet, then soaped, then rinsed and dried. I prefer to start at the top and work down. Surely each person develops his, or her, own procedure. Anyway, it seems to be a laborious endeavor. It is not nearly as satisfactory as a shower but, it is much better than nothing. Psychologically you have the satisfaction of having made a gallant attempt.

Early the following morning we heard a vehicle approaching! It turned out to be just what was needed. A big four-wheel drive Land-rover equipped with sand tires and a winch on the front! Two young men bailed out, one said, "Having a little trouble, are you?" The other unhooked the heavy wire from the wench and started the motor to unwind it. They stayed back away from the soft sand patch. In minutes the winch dragged the VW through the sand and out onto more firm ground.

As the wire was being re-wound we offered to pay them. They just laughed. "You OK now? Get in and see if it will start" As soon as it did they were back into their Land-Rover and off down the track. All we could do was yell "Thanks."

As we headed north toward El Golea we talked about them headed south into the teeth of the desert heat. How could they take it? We really wanted to make it to Tamanrasset but, we were driven out by the heat, wind, and sand. No matter, summer or winter, people, and other animals, are always moving about through the desert.

And, not only are people moving about through the desert. There is a Saharan Desert Ant that has evolved and adapted to living in the desert. (Cataglyphis) It is referred to by biologists as the premier thermopile. (Most heat-tolerant) It is able to forage with a body temperature of 123 F. It is able to stand surface sand temps of almost 160F. The ants emerge at such blistering temps and hunt for dead insects and arthropods that have expired due to the heat! By hunting for their food at such high temperatures they are escaping predation by other desert hunters. They are also able to move quickly which reduces their exposure to the heat.

The ants have long legs. Those legs raise them a short distance above the surface of the desert sand—and that may be just enough to keep them alive. "Ant height" on their relatively long legs may be about three eights of an inch but, it is enough to lower the temp of their bodies six to seven degrees. That could be the difference between life and death.

A German entomologist from the University of Ulm conducted experiments with the Saharan Desert ants. He glued pig bristles to their legs and then released them. He did not report that the increased height legated their foraging time, but, it did confuse them when they were returning to the nest. Changing the length of their legs scrambled the ant's internal pedometers. Those with lengthened legs traveled too far from the nest. When the legs were shortened they undershot the return trip. However, after a short time they readjusted their internal pedometers.

The Germans are conducting many interesting studies concerning the adaptation of plants and animals to the desert environment. One such study is attempting to understand exactly how the desert ants navigate. One explanation is that they are able to "count" the number of steps that they have taken. I do not think that idea is widely considered. The ants follow a very erratic path when foraging. Once they locate food that they are able to carry they follow an almost direct path on their return to the nest. To most researchers that indicates that the ants have a built-in navigation system similar to that of bees. It has been observed that while foraging the ants frequently look up at the sun, probably to orient themselves for the return trip to the nest. The bottom line is that, at present, their method of navigation is still a mystery.

Three genera of desert ants are known to have evolved in three different deserts around the world. This evolutionary adaptation has taken place in the Sahara in North Africa, the Namib Desert in south west Africa, and in the Australian Desert. All these ants are known to forage at temperatures above 140 F.

The Saharan desert ants are able to sustain an internal body temperature of 120 F.! These ants are active at, or near, the limit of animal potential. Again, it was the Germans who discovered that they are able to produce a special heat tolerant protein in their body cells. It is thought that the protein, in some fashion, provides them with the ability to withstand the excessive temps.

In spite of the heat Emma "volunteered" to help me look for ant nests. If you wish to obtain a better appreciation of what the ants are able to do, try crawling around on the hot sand trying to locate an opening to a nest. There are no "markers", they leave no surface indication as to where the nest is located. We had decided to give up the hunt and get back into the camper, out of the sun, and have some delicious hot water, when a lorry pulled up. He may have seen the two of us crawling about on the hot sand with our heads down

We were back in the camper with the side doors wide open. He remained in his lorry. There was no common language so we talked anyway, smiled, and did a lot of gesturing. He did not miss a thing! He saw our binoculars on the table and indicated that he would like to have them. Because he had a demanding attitude, I indicated that they were not for sale. When I turned down his offer of money, which was obviously not sincere, his demeanor changed. He raised his voice in what I considered a threatening manner, made several gestures which I had no way of interpreting and pounded on his steering wheel. It was best that we could not understand what he said in Arabic!

It was very hot, I was tired after our futile search for the ants, so it did not take much to make me angry. I thought that it would be best for me to act more aggressive. I stepped out of the camper and moved toward the lorry. I really had no idea as to what my next move should, or would, be. For what seemed to me to be a very long time but was probably only a few minutes, we stared at each other eyeball to eyeball. Without taking his eyes off me he suddenly switched on his motor and roared off into the distance, throwing up a cloud of sand. I made it back into the camper and Emma poured me a nice, refreshing, glass of hot water.

We did not sleep soundly that night. The night was spent sitting up and listening for the sound of an approaching lorry that never arrived. There were very few nights that we failed to fall asleep. The temp. during the day is excessive, but at night it gets quite cold, cold enough to freeze water! That morning we saw the sunrise.

When you see the sun rise over the Hamada, the plateau scoured by wind erosion, with sand dunes in the distance, the experience seems worth any hardships you have experienced. As the sun rises the shadows constantly shift and change. The warmth is welcome after the cold night—for a very brief few minutes. The heat starts to build almost at once as the sun climbs higher into the cloudless sky.

Back in the camper Emma made breakfast and we ate our oatmeal. Non-fat, dried milk certainly tastes delicious mixed with oatmeal!

It was a short run to Fort Mirabel. Why we thought that there would be a village near-by I do not know. The plain mud walls of the fort were located on a slight mound of rock and sand. It had been headquarters for a French Foreign brigade up until independence was gained by Algeria. Just below the fort was the dry bed of a wadi, a dry river. Scattered, struggling, desert bushes sent deep roots into the dry river bed seeking underground moisture. Although it does not rain frequently in the Sahara, when it does the downpour can be very severe. The wadi then becomes a raging torrent of rushing water tearing away, and carrying away, everything in its path.

Investigation of the fort revealed nothing! Everything that could be carried away had been. The large central compound was vacant, only the constant sound of the wind as it blew over the walls of the fort could be heard. The tiny cells where the troops had lived were empty and presented an atmosphere that was, even in the bright light of day, depressing. When we talked, and thought about, all the human activity that once took place within those walls, we actually lowered our voices. We tried to imagine what it had been like for a young trooper to have had to spend days, weeks, months, in this barren, forlorn location. And, usually, the fort was surrounded by tribes of resentful Arab desert tribesmen.

Several hours were spent searching the compound, the cells, and the area around the walls outside for anything that might have been left. Nothing was located. The sun was getting very hot, at least when we were in the camper there was some shade, and, even a slight breeze when we were moving. Even a hot breeze was better than none at all

The track north over the Plateau Du Tademait ran between two very large sand seas. On the east was the Grand Erg Oriental and, on the west the Grand Erg Occidental. These huge areas of sand dunes, unbroken by tracks or villages, cover many hundreds of square miles. They are almost completely free of any plant or animal life. During the thousands of years that people have inhabitant and traveled across the Sahara, these expanses of constantly shifting sand have been avoided.

Although they are completely without any form of any plant or animal life, they are fascinating to see. We drove the VW as close to the shifting dunes as we thought would be safe. Having been stranded, stuck in the sand for two days, and made us cautious. Not another vehicle was seen and, I think, that made us a little more nervous.

Two days were spent driving from one area to another. We were able to approach, but not enter, the vast expanse of sand. Some of the dunes were quite high, and they were difficult to climb, even on the windward surface where the sand was being blown upward to the crest. The leeward surface, or slip face as it is called, was more fun. The decent, where the wind-blown sand fell over the crest and slid down creating a cliff-like structure, formed an avalanche of sand when we descended over it. It was a great place to visit, as long as you had plenty of water and something to eat, even oatmeal, dried soup, beans, or sardines—With warm water!

Sand dunes are found all over the world. A large percentage of the earth's surface is sand, or, mixed sand and rock. Over-use by too many people has helped toward the expansion of most sand deserts. As the population has expanded the deserts have kept pace. The explosive population growth has not only expanded the desert, it has wiped-out many species of plants and animals that did manage to adapt to the arid desert conditions.

Sand dunes are great photographic subjects. They are constantly sculptured, and re-sculptured by the shifting winds. If the prevailing wind blows from one direction, the dune will form on any size obstruction. The obstruction might be a large or small rock, a bush, or tree. The sand will start to collect on the leeward side where the steep, or slip-face forms. The windward surface will be a gradual slope. Over time and a persistent wind from one direction, the dune will "walk" in the opposite direction from which the wind is blowing. That is what we saw in progress in Ain Salah. The "walking sand dune" slowly cutting the village in half! As was noted earlier, houses are covered by the advancing sand and uncovered as it recedes.

Sand is a formidable barrier! The Grand Ergs have prevented communication and trade for thousands of years. Tracks had to be created around them where more firm ground and water was available. The "Grand Plan" of the French to build a railroad across the Sahara to West Africa was not only prevented by the demand for freedom, it was also hampered by the desert sands. One writer said sand dunes are incredibly beautiful, thrilling, eerie, treacherous, or just plain inhospitable. Plants and animals that have been able to solve the problems involved from an evolutionary aspect, have developed the necessary characteristics required for survival under the most harsh environment on the planet.

There are three essential prerequisites required if sand dunes are to be formed—

1.  Obviously, and abundant supply of loose sand. An ancient lake bed, delta, or large depression into which the sand can be blown.
2.  A constant wind to supply the energy required to move the sand.
3.  A land area contoured in such fashion that the sand grains will lose their momentum. Shrubs, rocks, old dead trees or posts will obstruct the wind and cause the sand to pile up. It makes me think of snow drifts forming in the Pocono Mountains.

The closest snow drifts from the Grand Ergs would be in the Atlas Mountains to our west. From El Golea we planned to head west over the Atlas Mountains and back across Morocco to Casablanca where we might find a freighter heading for the east coast of the US.

The sand dunes in different parts of the world are composed of a variety of various weather-worn substances. The structure of the sand grains depends upon the mineral composition of the mountains that have been worn away. Most sand is composed of quartz and feldspar but gypsum, reef animals, sea shells, and even certain species of algae might be involved.

When we encountered a sand storm I worried about the abrasive action of the sand. Although most of the sand grains only travel a few feet above the surface of the ground, that is high enough to reach the wind-screen. The scouring action of the wind-driven sand can be observed on any structure exposed for any length of time. Also, when you are out in a sand storm you are very soon aware of what the blown sand is capable of doing to your skin. The Tuareg have ample reason to completely cover their face and all exposed areas. Those beautiful, indigo-dyed flowing blue robes are not worn for the sake of appearance.

The mechanics (physical) of wind-blown sand is too complicated for me. The form of the dunes, and the ripples formed on their wind-ward surface depends upon the size of the particles and the velocity of the wind. As was mentioned the direction from which the wind blows and its constancy are also important factors. Even the rotation of the planet is an important factor.

When Marco Polo traveled across the Gobi Desert he reported hearing strange sounds. He thought that the sounds were made by evil desert demons. Charles Darwin reported hearing strange desert sounds in the desert in Chile. The sounds have been reported as sounding like singing, whistling, squeaking, roaring, and booming. Others have reported kettle drums, artillery fire, thunder, low-flying planes, pipe organs, and violin music. We listened for such sounds but we did not hear anything.

It is presently thought that the sound is made by the sand grains falling down the slip-face of the dune. The moisture content must be just right. The size and velocity of the sand grains, and the underlying structure of the sand is involved. Some astronomers think that similar sounds might be created by the sand dunes on Mars!

The night before leaving the sand dune area a check of our maps indicated that we were just south of El Golea. Actually, our location was in the Grand Erg Occidental. Guardia, farther north was the location of the Mozabite villages and a better place to get any needed supplies. The decision was made to stop in El Golea for a day or so, pick up anything that might be required, then head on up to Ghardaia. The Tuareg make visits to Ghardaia and provide an opportunity to observe them once again.

That plan would require some back-tracking. The only track leading west in the region was one south of El Golea. It would take us over to Timimoun, north to Beni-Abbes, and on to Bechar. From Bechar it is a very short distance across the border to Figuig in Morocco. Our circuit of the Western Sahara would be complete!

Actually, it was more than a little disappointing to think that we would be leaving the Sahara, even with all the danger and hardships involved. The desert can be as beautiful and rewarding as it can be dangerous and cruel. The desert is like the ocean, one must plan carefully and enter with great caution and respect.

Well, enough nostalgia! We still had a lot of track to cover and interesting things to see, and people to observe. Maybe the best time to tell how great an adventure was is after you reach a safe place!

I checked the VW as best I could. Cleaned the oil and air filters, the fan belt that cooled the motor—It was worn and frayed! The valves were OK. There was no real shortage of water, fuel, oatmeal, canned meat, beans and sardines! The VW made its way over the rough track (the only type) headed north to El Golea.

The track into El Golea did not present any unexpected conditions. After some time driving over the desert you know that the tracks will vary from very bad to "not too bad" Almost all travelers going farther into the Sahara stop in El Golea, the last chance to obtain supplies before the 400 km. drive to Ain Salah. El Golea is about 300 km. south of the M'zab. The M'zab is a desolate area in which the Mozabites, a strict Moslem sect, settled almost a thousand years ago.

When we arrived in the oasis of El Golea it impressed us as a beautiful area. It made quite an impression on us after spending so many days crossing the Plateau De Tademait and the sand dunes of the Grand Erg Oriental. Our water tanks were low so it was essential that they be filled. I "tested" it by drinking some—After the saline water in Ain Salah it tasted very good. There were outside, public, spigots. It was not necessary to lower our folding canvass bucket down a well with a rope.

Emma found the outside market full of fresh vegetables and a variety of fruit. At some desert markets you buy dates—Or nothing! We were told that the oasis produces plums, cherries, oranges, figs, and apricots. I noticed that she did not buy any dates.

The grave of Charles de Foucauld is located here, about one thousand miles north of his hermitage in the Hoggar Mountains. We thought that he would have preferred being buried there in the mountains where he spent so many years. "Well," I said to Emma, "once you are dead you have no control over what happens." We did not go to visit it. Isabella Eberhardt was buried in El-Oued on the western edge of the Grand Erg oriental. We did not visit her grave either. Although we respected these two very different individuals very much for what they did while alive, we do not feel that a visit to their grave sites would change anything. To us, what is important is to attempt to understand their missions, their philosophies of life and living.

There was a small airport in El Golea with infrequent flights to Algiers and Tamanrasset. We were told that getting a seat was not a sure thing. The over-land desert buss also stops here. They are often very crowded, hot, and rough-riding. Experienced riders have reported that, a journey across the desert in one of those busses, driven by an Arab, can be a real adventure. While en route, facilities are limited to those available in the open desert. When a halt is absolutely required, the buss stops. The men are supposed to go off to one side of the bus the right side, the women the opposite side. We have been witness to several of these procedures. Be advised that under such circumstances, the desert provides no privacy. The Arab women with their voluminous flowing robes are at an advantage, women with short skirts are on their own!

Women traveling alone should use caution in boarding desert busses or cabs. Many Arab men seem to have some distorted ideas with respect to women from the US or Europe. Friends of ours from Denmark had an exciting time attempting to travel across the desert in a crowded cab. They were seated next to each other in the back seat of the cab. An Arab man sat next to the husband. Apparently he was so attracted to the woman that he attempted to crawl across her husband in order to reach her!

There was a scuffle in the cab while the Dane tried to fend off the amorous Arab. The result was that the cab stopped in the desert and the Danish couple found themselves Stranded! Fortunately, a passing lorry stopped and brought them safely into the village.

As mentioned earlier, Isabella Eberhardt traveled throughout the Sahara during the late eighteen hundreds. She dressed as a man, rode horseback, and lived a very fast life. Everyone knew that she was a woman, still, the Arab men accepted her as a man. I have never been able to learn just how she accomplished that—And I do not think that just because Isabella got away with it, other women can.

El Golea seemed more "open" to us. While wandering about we did not get that "closed in "feeling." Most Arab houses are walled-in with open courtyards in the center. The outside walls are mud bricks and plastered over, unpainted and undecorated. The passages between buildings are narrow, unpaved, sandy and dusty. The central courtyard can be very beautiful. Several that we visited were lined with decorative tile, walls and floors. Often, in the center there is a decorative fountain, also lined with colorful tile. Of course, while the designs may be very colorful and pleasing, no animal life is portrayed, that is forbidden by the Koran.

Emma and I, when staying in an Arab home, thought that the bathroom life a bit to be desired. There always seems to be a ceramic bowl and pitcher of water that you would really like to take with you. The bowl and water are for washing the left hand, the one used by Arabs for cleaning themselves after a bowel movement. That body function is carried out over a hole in the floor about six inches in diameter. Personally, I found aiming my rear end accurately, was quite a challenge! I can not say that it was a procedure in which I had no interest. However, it was one that I did fail to pursue.

When you are an invited guest in an Arab home you are treated like royalty. (Actually, I have no idea as to how royalty is treated.) We were usually served cous cous, a ground meal of grain, mixed with fresh vegetables and lamb. It was always delicious. The main meal is followed by sweet cakes, hot tea, also very sweet, with mint. Oranges, right from the tree, tops it off!

My problem was eating the stew. The right hand is used with the fingers forming a scoop. The food is packed into a ball and pushed, or catapulted, into your mouth. Once you acquire the knack of the procedure it is very easy. The large bowl of food was placed in the middle with all the guests sitting, squat-legged around it. The carpet covering the tiled floor was very attractive, thick, and comfortable. We found it to be a most enjoyable experience. (Then reality—Back to the VW, and stew)

In the bar, which was quiet and pleasant, the only part of the hotel that we saw, we were told that about 14,000 people live in El Golea. The bar tender also reported that there are 200,000 palm trees in the oasis. I did not think it appropriate that I inquire as to the accuracy of those figures. We did see many palm trees and a lot of people. There were also some pines and eucalyptuses trees scattered about. It was a very pleasant change from the Hammada and the Grand Erg Occidental, which, by the way, seemed to possibly be approaching from the west.

On one hill overlooking the white village an old ruined Ksar was located. We did not attempt to investigate it but it appeared to have seen better days. One swan and a few wild ducks were swimming about in a rather small brackish lake. There were more ducks on a long lake or body of water just out of the village. No other animals were seen.

A couple miles out of the village, along the track there was a white church with two towers. It appeared to be in need of repair and some paint. A group of Catholic nuns occupy the building. In side there were paintings of several saints done by Charles de Foucauld. Foucauld was buried here in 1929. As mentioned earlier, we felt that if he had anything to say about it, he would have selected the Hoggar Mountains where he built his, now famous, Hermitage. The church and cemetery have received little, or no, attention since the end of the French occupation.

The Arabs are Moslems. From what we saw and heard the vast majority of them plan to remain Moslems. The Berbers across North Africa accepted the Moslem religion whole-heartedly. They were converted to Moslem beliefs and the authority of the Koran long before the actual Arab Conquest. Children are indoctrinated by being taught from the Koran long before they are able to think, let alone reason. The situation is very similar to that in the US with respect to the Bible.

Ghardaia was our nest objective, about 320 kilometers to the north. We had decided that under the circumstances in the north with respect to shootings and bombings, it would be wiser, and safer, not to go there.

Everything is relative, the road from El Golea to Ghardaia seemed quite good, compared to the tracks we had been over. It wound around some broken edges of the more extensive plateau to the east. The Grand Erg Oriental formed a huge sea of sand covering thousands of square miles some miles to our right. (East as we drove north.) There were no obstacles to deal with. No steep mountains, passes, sharp curves, or dangerous unguarded, rock and sand-covered sections to negotiate. In a way, I was a little disappointed. Emma was not.

Ghardaia is located on the Chaka Plain, a desolate, remote, rock-strewn area. The type terrain that only fugitives, or the persecuted, would attempt to inhabit. And the five villages that presently make up Ghardaia were founded by a fanatic sect of the Moslem faith driven out of the north. A winding green ravine breaks the desolation of the barren, rock-strewn Chebka. All the stones and cement used in the construction of the houses and mosques were collected locally.

The green valley, about six miles long, provided a refuge for the persecuted Mozabites. There were original inhabitants, very few of them who had migrated from the north on their own many years before the Mozabites.

History records people living in the valley of the Mzab, as the valley is called, about 800 AD. About a hundred years later the Mozabites began to arrive from the north. It was the Mozabites who built the five villages from the raw material available locally. Conservation was the operative word. Nothing was wasted.

Thick walls around each house maintain the desired privacy desired from the outside world, even the streets. No structure could be built higher than the mosque. The mosque was constructed at the highest point and, it was surrounded by a public square. The mosque was not decorated in any way. It tapered from the bottom toward the top in which there were openings through which the muzzin called the faithful to prayer five times each day.

The conservative, austere, architecture demanded by the Mozabites beliefs resulted in buildings that blended into the natural environment. After visiting one very attractive home Emma said, "When we get home we should build our house on the Arab plan." I agreed. We were never able to do it. When you are in the courtyard of an Arab home, decorated by pleasant colored tiles of geometric designs, isolated from the sound and sights of the society outside, there is a unique atmosphere and peacefulness, your entire body and mind seems to relax. The Arabs discovered, and began to practice, more than a thousand years ago, and a way of life that is incomprehensible to the modern American society.

All life is dependant upon water. The Mozabites, along the usually dry river bed in the Chabka Plain were no exception. Water had to be found.

The answer was to dig wells and, we were informed, dig they did. Wells were dug as deep as 200 feet! We have no concept of the back-breaking labor involved. The water was there but, the river was flowing deep underground! The water from the more shallow wells could be brought to the surface with a balance pole. A pole balanced on a fulcrum that lowered a sheep skin bucket down into the water. The water was stored in a mud tank lined with lime and then run through channels to the crops. The energy required could be supplied by a man. However, on the deepest wells, donkeys or camels had to be employed. The mechanism used sliding cords and pulleys, I did not understand what the man was telling us.

There are now some 50,000 Mozabites living in the area of the Mzab. There is not enough water for that size population. Many new wells have been dug, water towers have been erected and pipes laid. Perhaps deep wells can be drilled and diesel pumps used if an underground aquifer is located. No matter, the bottom line is that the ultimate supply of water is finite—Population growth, allowed to expand uncontrolled because of ancient religious beliefs, appears to be infinite. It is a recipe for disaster!

When we were there we were told by some of the younger generation that they are being forced to leave. They are intelligent and they are very good business people. We got the impression that the men move north and start various business enterprises. They maintain their families at home. When they have been successful and saved enough money, they return. We found the same thing being practiced in Greece.

On top of the mosques, and on graves in the cemetery, there were what appeared to be earthen balls and finger-like projections. The crescent moon appeared on some decorations. Obviously they have religious significance but, we were not able to discover exactly what it might be.

The market place in central Ghardaia was, we thought, the most interesting. It was the center of activity. The Mozabites are very strict Moslems, they have gone to great lengths to protect their privacy and their way of life. Their homes are constructed in order to maintain that privacy. It was about the only place that we were really able to see the people in action.

The men are more out-going, seem to be more informed, especially the younger generation. In the market several men spoke English very well. We did not find any women who spoke at all. An "equal rights law," was passed but we did not see any indication that it was being enforced.

The variety of items for sale would be difficult to describe. Most of it was "traditional". things used locally by the people. But, we were surprised that a great number of things were "modern", imported from the north. There were piles of aluminum pots and pans, and racks of manufactured clothes. We got the impression that although the Mozabites are very strict Moslems, they are also very clever business men.

The men were very active and moved around, most of the women sat quietly, usually on the ground, behind whatever they were selling. The women were completely covered from head to foot by their flowing robes. Their heads were shrouded by yards of cloth that exposed only one eye. They appeared to be able to conduct their business very efficiently with that one eye.

On several occasions we saw a Tuareg ride into the square. We never saw two of them together. Their visits were very brief. Every one that we saw rode a big, beautiful, white camel. The animal appeared to be well cared for and well-trained. When a Tuareg rode in everyone stepped back, they seemed to exhibit an attitude of authority. Anyway, they were respected. They were very impressive. The camel seemed able to respond to what the rider was thinking—But it was, no doubt, his body movement.

One of the merchants must have seen us watching the scene of the Tauregs entry, brief stay, and departure. He walked over and started to tell us about the Tuareg people. He seemed to be well informed with respect to their history, background, and current problems. I will try to briefly summarize what he said—And add some current research in an attempt to bring the account a little more up to date—

The Tuareg are a nomadic pastoralist people. They inhabit, and have inhabited, the interior and southern areas of the Sahara. They do not refer to themselves as being "tuareg", that name was coined by early explorers. They call themselves the Kel. They also refer to themselves as "the free people" and, "the people of the veil." The estimate as to their population varies around one million. Tuareg tribes are found in Niger, Mali, Algeria, Burkina Faso, and Libya. These countries were drawn on a map by the French with no consideration of the tribes living there. That thoughtless act has caused untold suffering and the death of millions of indigenous natives.

Now most Tuareg live in West Africa. Formerly they roamed throughout the entire Sahara Desert. It is thought that the Tuareg descended from ancient Berber tribes. Some authorities feel that the Tuareg language indicates an ancient Berber origin. For more than two thousand years they controlled everything that crossed the desert on the five main caravan routes. The camel, "the ship of the desert", was introduced to the Sahara from Saudi Arabia about two thousand years ago. I thought that was interesting.

The Tuareg, in the past, took captives. They were trained to become servants and herdsmen. Some were held for ransom, some were sold. The practice of taking captives for various purposes was common throughout Africa. Some of the Chiefs sold captured people to slave traders from Europe. Those slaves ended up in a great number of countries. Outlawed in many countries, slavery, in a variety of forms, is still widely practiced. As mentioned earlier, the former slave market place is still being used in Ain Salah—But not, so far as we could learn, to sell slaves.

As a result of the French divisions, local conflicts have erupted in many countries. Some of the fighting was an effort by local Tuareg tribes to gain independence, some of it has been over sharing the money from the exploitation of natural resources.

The damage done by foreign politician's lives on long after they are dead and disintegrating in their graves. That has, and is happening, all over the world. I have been most concerned when I see it happening, over and over, in the US.

There broad swords were no match for the more advanced French weapons. Thousands were killed on both sides but, the French prevailed and the Tuareg Confederations were dismantled, divided, and reorganized. The original Tuareg Society never recovered.

Whenever a "more advanced society", whatever that might be, contacts a, "more primitive society, or culture," the two can not co-exist. The best example of that took place in the US where the Europeans did their very best to exterminate the native population which had lived in the area for thousands of years.

Current problems have exacerbated Tuareg problems. They include, French restrictions on nomadic, rampant population growth, desertification, global warming, need for firewood, and water shortages. The younger generation is experimenting with farming but, it is very difficult for them to alter their way of life and, farming in a drought-stricken area is almost impossible. As a result many are moving into villages, towns, and cities in order to find jobs. That spells the end of the traditional Tuareg way of life.

Because of uncontrolled population growth, and the hysteria for globalization, there is no room left for the natural world of life upon which, ultimately, all life depends. And man was named Homo sapiens, (wise man).) "Boobus stupidensis" would have been much more appropriate.

That merchant was very intelligent. I am certain that he could have told us a lot more But, his business was unattended and, we were not cash-customers. We had no desire to terminate the conversation. We felt most fortunate that he gave us so much time and, first-hand information. He left us with a lot to think over, and talk about.

After several days wandering about the Ghardaia area we decided that it was about time to think of heading back toward Morocco, Casablanca, a freighter, and the US. Our funds were getting rather limited and, since there was little possibility of getting any additional support from home, we decided the best course of action would be to return to the US, locate a new teaching position, save our money for five years, and plan another trip to Africa!.

# THE END
*By Ted Jones and Emma Selig Jones*